Companion to

The Plough and the Stars

Patrick Murray

The Educational Company of Ireland

First published 1986
This reprint 1995

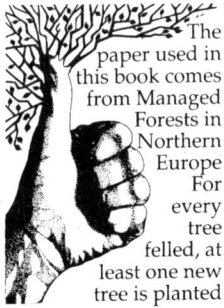

The
paper used in
this book comes
from Managed
Forests in
Northern
Europe
For
every
tree
felled, at
least one new
tree is planted

The Educational Company of Ireland
Ballymount Road
Walkinstown
Dublin 12

A trading unit of Smurfit Services Limited

Approved Quality
System

Cover Photograph: Vapron Productions, 1989. Direction by Joe Dowling
with Catherine Byrne as Nora Clitheroe and Aedin Moloney as Mollser.

Design and Typesetting by Phototype-Set Ltd, Glasnevin, Dublin.
Proofreading: S. Donohoe.

Printed in the Republic of Ireland by Citiprint Ltd., Dublin

Contents

NOTE: All references to the play are taken from
The Plough and the Stars
(Gill and Macmillan, Dublin 1987).

The Dramatist

SEÁN O'Casey was born John Casey in Dorset Street, Dublin on 30 March 1880. At the time of Seán's birth, his father, Michael Casey, was a clerk with the Irish Church Missions, a Protestant action group; his mother came from a staunchly Protestant Wicklow family. His father was a well-read, scholarly man, whose library contained numerous religious works, several versions of the Bible, and the standard English poetic and dramatic classics. O'Casey's father died in 1886. His death marked the decline of the family's fortunes, but although the O'Caseys lived thereafter in genteel poverty, they never had to endure the squalid tenement life depicted in *The Plough and the Stars*.

EARLY INFLUENCES

Seán's schooling was irregular. He suffered from a debilitating eye disease, but developed a remarkable ability to commit to memory many passages from books read to him by his mother and older sister. These memorised passages, particularly the biblical ones, are used to advantage in the plays. In *The Plough and the Stars*, for example, the speeches of Bessie Burgess contain many biblical echoes. At the age of fourteen, Seán began work as a store-assistant. He was dismissed from his first two jobs for insubordination and impertinence. Later, at the age of twenty-three, he found employment as a labourer with the Great Northern Railway, from which he was dismissed after eight years for refusing to sign a document undertaking not to join Jim Larkin's Irish Transport and

General Workers' Union. Following a period of unemployment which brought him real hardship, he found temporary work as a builder's labourer.

O'Casey's life took a surprising course for a member of a lower-middle-class Protestant family. In his early twenties he joined the Drumcondra branch of the Gaelic League, gaelicised his name to Seán O'Cathasaigh, and learned the Irish language with the aid of Father O'Growney's *Simple Lessons in Irish*. He joined the GAA and soon afterwards the IRB. He played hurling despite his weak eyesight. He helped to found the St. Laurence O'Toole Piper's Band. His religious faith was weakened by his study of Darwin's *Descent of Man*, and by some shattering family experiences. In 1911, he joined Jim Larkin's union, and soon began writing letters and articles for Larkin's paper, *The Irish Worker*. He tried to forge an alliance between the Gaelic League, the IRB and the Labour movement, but when the nationalist bodies rejected this idea, he resigned from both the Gaelic League and the IRB. From this point onwards, he became increasingly disenchanted with middle-class nationalism, a disenchantment reflected in *The Plough and the Stars*.

In the Great Strike of 1913, Seán O'Casey acted as secretary of the Strikers' Relief Committee. When the Citizen Army, founded by Larkin to protect workers from attack, was reorganised in 1914, O'Casey was made its honorary secretary. When Larkin's successor, James Connolly, led the Labour movement in a nationalist direction and formed an alliance with Pearse and the more militant members of the Irish Volunteers who were planning an armed rising, O'Casey became disillusioned. He dissociated himself from the Citizen Army and the Volunteers, and took no part in the 1916 Rising. The notion of an armed struggle against the British occupation of Ireland became increasingly repugnant to him, although he still believed in Irish independence, if this could be achieved by peaceful methods. Despite his breach with the Citizen Army, he wrote its history, which appeared in 1919. The small fee which he received for the manuscript helped to pay his mother's funeral expenses. It did not, however, help to pay her medical expenses, as O'Casey recalled with much bitterness in his autobiographical reminiscences:

> — She's a very old woman, the doctor remarked, very old, and tired too. The pulse is weak; very weak; and he stood, staring at the still figure on the sofa — waiting for the fee, Seán thought bitterly.
> — I can't give you five shillings just now, he said aloud, flushing crimson, for a cheque I got hasn't been cashed yet.
> — Cheque? The doctor was startled. What cheque would you have? and he set his soft hat firmly on his head, looking searchingly into Seán's face.
> — One I got for writing a book, said Seán; it's to be published soon.
> — A book? Indeed? Well, the next time you haven't a fee handy, get the Dispensary doctor, please; that's what he's for — to attend to you people. And without another word he left the house, without telling Seán what was to be done for his mother.
>
> *(Inishfallen, Fare Thee Well)*

O'CASEY, A CONTROVERSIAL PLAYWRIGHT

Experiences like this one deeply influenced O'Casey's dramatic writing.

In 1919, he attended the Abbey theatre production of *Blight,* a play by Oliver St. John Gogarty dealing with the appalling conditions in the Dublin slums. This seems to have given him the idea that he could do something similar based on his own knowledge and experience of the lives of the Dublin poor. He submitted a few plays to the Abbey, which were rejected, but in 1922, his two-act play, *On the Run,* was accepted, and presented as *The Shadow of a Gunman* in 1923. This was followed in 1924 by *Juno and the Paycock,* which has a Civil War setting, and which is generally regarded as his best play, and *The Plough and the Stars* (1926) which deals with the Easter Rising of 1916. With the success of these plays, O'Casey was at last a professional writer, able to live on his earnings from literary work. Although *The Plough and the Stars* was an outstanding artistic and commercial success, O'Casey was disturbed by the personal hostility of some of the Abbey actors, and by various attempts to censor the play. When he was asked to go to London to promote a production of *Juno and the Paycock* he agreed. In 1926, he left Dublin to settle in London. Later, when the Abbey rejected his experimental play, *The Silver Tassie,* he described himself as 'a voluntary and settled exile from every creed, from every party, and from every literary clique in Ireland.' In 1927 he married the Irish actress Eileen Carey.

O'Casey's three best plays are the 'realistic' ones he wrote before his exile: *The Shadow of a Gunman, Juno and the Paycock* and *The Plough and the Stars*. These are the last great masterpieces of the Abbey Theatre. His later plays, after *The Silver Tassie,* which was first produced in London in 1929, are experimental, symbolic and propagandist. The most important of these are: *Within the Gates* (1934); *The Star Turns Red* (1940); *Purple Dust* (1945); *Red Roses for Me* (1946); *Oak Leaves and Lavender* (1947); *Cock-a-Doodle Dandy* (1949); *The Bishop's Bonfire* (1955); *The Drums of Father Ned* (1958). The last two plays satirise the Irish clergy and middle classes.

In his exile, from 1926 until his death in 1964, O'Casey was a stern critic of what he conceived to be the faults of Irish society. His most powerful criticism of the country he still loved is found in the six volumes of his autobiographical reminiscences, which appeared from 1939 until 1954, and which chronicle O'Casey's career from childhood to his triumph as a dramatist, in the process striking powerful blows at a wide variety of persons and institutions.

O'CASEY, THE ESPOUSER OF CAUSES

O'Casey and his work are full of contradictions. There are, in particular, some remarkable inconsistencies between what he says about himself in his autobiography, and the facts as established by scholarly research. In his autobiography, he gives the clear impression that he was a working-class rebel, a child of the Dublin slums. He was, in fact, born into a cultured, respectable, lower-middle-class family, whose members, with the exception of Seán himself, attended a fee-paying school. He was liable to be wildly enthusiastic about whatever cause he espoused at a particular period, but Desmond Ryan was not far wrong when he remarked that O'Casey's mind could hold only one enthusiasm at a time. His early interest in the Protestant religion of his childhood was totally absorbing. He spoke at prayer meetings, supported the foreign missions, taught Sunday School, and applied himself diligently to biblical study. When he abandoned religion, he became for a time a dedicated supporter of the Irish-Ireland movement. His subsequent career is a record of progressive disillusionment with every major cause to which he attached himself. As C. Desmond Greaves points out, O'Casey 'broke with the IRB because it would not commit its military force to the defence of the locked-out workers. He was bitterly opposed to the Volunteers because, since their leaders included employers, he thought they must be antagonistic to the working-class at every point. He broke with the Citizen Army because it permitted Countess Markiewicz to continue her association with Cumann Na mBan, which O'Casey considered a middle-class organisation'.

His break with the Citizen Army meant that he took no part in the 1916 Rising. He afterwards claimed that he was opposed to the Rising when it took place, and in *The Plough and the Stars* he takes a less than flattering look at those who instigated and took part in it. But in October 1917, in his first independently-published work, a broadside on his friend the patriot Thomas Ashe, who had died after a lengthy hunger-strike, O'Casey glorifies the Rising. He tended to respond emotionally and personally to issues and ideas; he was not a stable or coherent thinker. In the early nineteen-thirties, he professed a vague, benevolent form of communism. In 1937 he proclaimed himself a Marxist, and became an extravagant admirer of the USSR. This, his last political creed, which commanded his loyalty longer than any other, involved him in further contradictions. He was a deeply compassionate man, but, as D.E.S. Maxwell points out, 'In a sad paradox, proclaiming himself a proletarian communist, his eyes never opened to the perversions of Stalinism'.

Early Reactions to The Plough and the Stars

'BEYOND THE BEYONDS'

WHEN, in August 1925, O'Casey submitted *The Plough and the Stars* to the directors of the Abbey Theatre, they accepted it unanimously. However, the producer, M. J. Dolan, and many of the actors, had grave reservations about the play, mainly on moral grounds. When rehearsals began under Dolan's direction, serious problems arose. Dolan disliked both O'Casey and his play, and after reading the script he wrote a strongly critical letter to Lady Gregory setting forth his objections. 'At any time', he complained, 'I would think twice about having anything to do with it. The language in it is — to use an Abbey phrase — beyond the beyonds. The song at the end of the Second Act, sung by the girl in the streets — is unpardonable'. Dolan also persuaded Dr George O'Brien, the government nominee on the Board of Directors of the Abbey Theatre, to demand substantial changes in the script. In particular, O'Brien argued that the love scene in Act One between Nora and Jack did not ring true; that the part of Rosie Redmond 'could not possibly be allowed to stand', and that her song at the end of Act Two was 'outrageous'. He also demanded that numerous offending words and phrases throughout the play be changed. If his demands were not met, he feared that public indignation might lead to the withdrawal of the government subsidy to the Abbey. Yeats and the other directors conceded that the love scene contained implausible passages, and they agreed to the excision of the love-song.

Some of the actors had their own misgivings about the play. Eileen Crowe, who was to play Mrs. Gogan, refused to speak the lines 'any kid, livin' or dead, that Jinnie Gogan's had since, was got between th' bordhers of th' Ten Commandments!' (Act 2, lines 380-82). When O'Casey asked her why she wouldn't play Mrs. Gogan, she told him that the part was not 'genteel'. She had to be replaced. F. J. McCormick, who was married to Eileen Crowe, refused to use the word 'snotty'. Some of the members of the cast tried to persuade Ria Mooney not to play the part of Rosie Redmond because, as she recalled, 'They felt they would be besmirched by the fact of one of them playing such a role.'

RIOTING IN THE ABBEY

The first performance of the play on 8 February 1926 went off without incident before a capacity audience. Three nights afterwards, however, a planned demonstration by nationally-minded people led to a riot in the theatre. The entire performance was interrupted by the shouting and singing of members of the audience, mostly women. Some of these women were relatives of the men who had died in the 1916 Rising, among them the mother of Padraig Pearse and the widow of Tom Clarke, who objected to O'Casey's treatment of the Rising. They took particular exception to Nora Clitheroe's description of the fighting in the streets in Act Three. O'Casey recalled the demonstration with his characteristic mockery of those who did not like his work: 'The high, hysterical distorted voices of women kept squealing that Irish girls were noted over the whole world for their modesty, and that Ireland's name was holy; that the Republican flag had never seen the inside of a public house; that this slander on the Irish race would mean the end of the Abbey Theatre; and that Ireland was Ireland through joy and tears.' O'Casey remembered Barry Fitzgerald, who was playing Fluther, entering into the spirit of the part by 'sending an enemy, who had climbed onto the stage, flying into the stalls with a Flutherian punch on the jaw.'

Yeats, the senior director of the Abbey Theatre, was on the whole rather pleased with the demonstration against the play. He was smiling broadly as he arrived in the theatre to make a speech condemning the demonstrators. He clearly had advance knowledge of the fact that a problem was going to arise, since he had, before going to the theatre, given a copy of his speech to *The Irish Times*. Having sent for the police, Yeats spoke from the stage amid a continuing uproar. As he spoke, he recalled the rioting that had accompanied an early performance of Synge's *Playboy of the Western World* in 1907. 'You have', he told the hostile audience at O'Casey's play 'disgraced yourselves again. Is this to be an ever-recurring celebration of the arrival of Irish genius? Synge first and then O'Casey. The news of the happening of the last few minutes will go from country to country. Dublin has rocked the cradle of genius. From such a scene in this theatre went forth the fame of Synge. Equally the fame of O'Casey is born here to-night. This is his apotheosis!'

In spite of these stirring words of Yeats, critical reaction to *The Plough and the Stars* was not very much more favourable than that of the actors or the members of the audience. Liam O'Flaherty condemned it as a bad play. The respected critic Andrew E. Malone found it seriously flawed, suggesting that O'Casey was striving 'after a literary quality of speech which is entirely alien to the Dublin slum-dwellers' and that all his plays were 'a series of scenes rather than organic works.' Malone also believed that O'Casey had dealt with 'abnormal and transient' phases of Dublin life. Austin Clarke, the poet and dramatist, argued that O'Casey's work was a 'crude exploitation of our poorer people'. The hostility of the reception given to *The Plough and the Stars* was a major factor in O'Casey's decision to leave Ireland and settle in England.

Analysis and Commentary

ACT 1

THE TENEMENT BACKGROUND

THE setting of the first Act is the home of Jack and Nora Clitheroe, a young married couple who share a seedy Dublin tenement with Nora's uncle, Peter Flynn, a labourer; Jack's cousin, The Young Covey, a fitter; Bessie Burgess, a fruit-vendor; Mrs. Gogan, a charwoman and her consumptive daughter Mollser; and Fluther Good, a carpenter. The year is 1916. The quality of Dublin slum-life in that year is powerfully evoked by O'Casey in this play and in many passages of his autobiographical reminiscences. The following extract from the latter conveys the dismal atmosphere of the endless rows of tenement buildings in which working-class families such as the Clitheroes spent their lives:

> There were the houses too — a long, lurching row of discontented incurables, smirched with the age-long marks of ague, fevers, cancer and consumption, the soured tears of little children, and the sighs of disappointed newly married girls. The doors were scarred with time's spit and anger's hasty knocking: the pillars by their sides were shaky, their stuccoed bloom long since peeled away, and they looked like crutches keeping trembling doors standing on their palsied feet. The gummy-eyed windows blinked dimly out, lacquered by a year's tired dust from the troubled street below. Dirt and disease were the big sacraments here — outward and visible signs of an inward and spiritual disgrace.

INTEREST IN POLITICAL ISSUES

Even against such a background, most of the characters in *The Plough and the Stars* contrive to conquer despair, to preserve a remarkable exuberance and buoyancy of temper, and to maintain a lively interest in the great political and social issues of the day as well as in the smallest details of everyday life.

We learn a good deal about Nora Clitheroe, the principal female character, even before she comes on stage. The incurably inquisitive Mrs. Gogan cannot resist opening a parcel for Nora from Arnotts containing an expensive hat. This detail, together with Mrs. Gogan's comment on Nora's fondness for rather daring attire and her insistence on preserving the conventions of common politeness, define her as a woman with pretensions and ambitions beyond those commonly found among the residents of the tenement. She is, as a later stage-direction confirms, 'a little anxious to get on in the world' (lines 466-7).

Mrs. Gogan now introduces one of the central themes of the play: the changing and deteriorating relationship between Nora and her husband Jack. As Mrs. Gogan sees it, their once ardent love has cooled considerably. Fluther speculates, quite misleadingly as it happens, whether Jack may be attracted to another woman. It soon transpires that the Citizen Army is Nora's rival for Jack's attentions. Nora, the model housewife, is not content to live much longer in a tenement house. Her reason, as reported by Mrs. Gogan, forms one of the many striking pieces of social comment in the play; tenements are 'vaults that are hidin' th' dead, instead of homes that are shelterin' th' livin''.

VARIOUS SHADES OF NATIONALISM

As Peter Flynn prepares for his patriotic meeting in Parnell Square, we are introduced to the political theme. Peter, a member of a patriotic organisation known as The Foresters, will be among those marching to honour the memory of Irish patriots. Peter is more a figure of fun than a man with serious heroic pretensions: his main patriotic endeavour is to dress up in an absurdly antique uniform, to march to Wolfe Tone's grave, and to express his love of Ireland in the empty rhetoric with which The Covey taunts him ('Dear harp o' me counthry, in darkness I found thee...' line 452).

Peter Flynn represents a type of romantic nationalism that is harmless, ineffectual, nostalgic and sentimental. Jack Clitheroe's dedication to the cause of Irish freedom is much more serious and determined. He is a member of the Irish Citizen Army, and has been expecting to be made one of its officers. The apparent disappointment of these hopes has embittered him. The serious business of Clitheroe's disenchantment is temporarily interrupted by a comic interlude involving Mrs. Gogan and Fluther (lines 222-83). Mrs. Gogan, noticing that Fluther has a slight cold, contrives to make him believe that it may well prove fatal: her references to sudden death and funerals, and her display of Peter's shroud-like shirt induce symptoms of illness in Fluther, whose own explanation is characteristically comic ('I feel as dizzy as bedamned! I hope I didn't give up the beer too suddenly', lines 283-4).

The Plough and the Stars is a drama of ideas, the most serious of which get only a very tentative hearing. Peter Flynn represents romantic nationalism and Jack Clitheroe the growing physical force movement. The Covey, whose ideas are close to those of O'Casey himself, has no time for nationalism of any kind, or for the ancient Irish pieties: he is a doctrinaire socialist, serious and somewhat tiresome in his views, much given to quoting from left-wing thinkers, and feeling the utmost contempt for the endeavours of the Citizen Army, which by 1916 had become more nationalist and less socialist than it had been at its foundation. The Covey sees nationalism as a dangerous enemy of human progress. His view is that men should lay stress not on national differences but on their common humanity. ('Look here, comrade, there's no such thing as an Irishman, or an Englishman, or a German or a Turk, we're all only human bein's', lines 314-6). The Covey is also much influenced by the materialistic interpretation of the universe, and is familiar with popular versions of Darwin's teachings. He rejects religion as well as nationalism, sweeping aside the idea of divine creation with the assertion that human existence is 'all a question of the accidental gatherin' together of mollycewels an' atoms' (lines 317-8), and that the ancestral claims of Adam and Eve must give way to those of 'th' man o' Java' (line 358). The seriousness of The Covey's discourse on such ultimate issues as God and creation is somewhat undercut by Peter's angry comments on the difficulties he is experiencing with his stiff collar. The constant juxtaposition of the serious with the trivial is the source of much of the comedy in *The Plough and the Stars*.

Fluther's contribution to the debate is a rhetorical one. He describes The Covey as 'a worum' and 'a little ignorant yahoo of a red flag socialist'. He resents The Covey's rejection of religion, and enjoys the prospect of contemplating his opponent 'kickin' an' yellin' for a priest on his death-bed'. Fluther himself is an upholder of established institutions.

The weakest passage in the Act is the farcical episode involving The Covey and Peter (lines 407-520). The conflict between the two, which has its basis in political differences, is mainly a matter of strident verbal abuse involving the excessive use of alliteration ('It's a nice thing to have a lunatic like this lashin' around with a lethal weapon'; I'll make him stop his laughin' an' leerin', jibin' an' jeerin'). Violent threats and gestures are made on both sides without serious intent; it is a relief when Nora brings the tedious episode to an end. Her main concern is that the behaviour of The Covey and Peter is not in keeping with the 'respectable home' she is striving to establish. The Covey's line in crude verbal abuse ('you lemon-whiskered oul' swine') is at odds with his pretensions to philosophical detachment and his fondness for such ponderous titles as *Thesis on th' Origin, Development an' Consolidation of th' Evolutionary Idea of th' Proleteriat.*

With the entry of Bessie Burgess (line 545) we meet perhaps the most colourful and compelling character in the play. Bessie is a shrewish, tough, coarse-tongued, earthy woman, aggressive to a fault, given to speaking her mind freely, lacking in tact and sensitivity. Bessie has an important function in the political scheme of the play. She represents the very considerable body of Irish people who favoured the British cause during the First World War; her son is in the trenches fighting the Germans.

Jack Clitheroe is the last of the principal characters to be introduced. O'Casey, in a significant stage-direction, indicates an unfavourable contrast between Jack's character and his wife's. Jack's face, we are told, 'has none of the strength of Nora's. It is a face in which is the desire for authority without the power to attain it'. The first outward sign of conflict between Jack and Nora is apparent when she firmly rejects his idea that they should both go to the political meeting (line 624). Jack is envious of Brennan the chicken-butcher, who has been made an officer in the Citizen Army, the rank he himself aspired to. The short exchange between Jack and The Covey on the new role of the Citizen Army is highly significant. The Covey, expressing O'Casey's point of view, thinks that those who use the flag bearing the plough and the stars for political purposes are disgracing it. The Covey argues that this flag is essentially a communist banner to be used only 'when we're buildin' the barricades to fight for a workers' republic'. It is, in other words, the emblem of the working-classes in their struggle against capitalism, and for 'Ireland's warriors' to exploit it as a political and nationalistic emblem is to insult the cause it really represents.

JACK AND NORA, LOVE AND CONFLICT

The scene between Jack and Nora, after the others have left, has some notable features. Most people tend to find it embarrassing for its mawkish sentimentality. The small-talk of the two is trivial and repetitious ('Little, little, red-lipped Nora'), but in this it can be said to reflect many real-life situations of the same kind. The most notable feature of this scene is its suggestion of uneasiness in both parties about the nature of their relationship. Jack is clearly restless, and would like to be at the meeting. Nora is doing all she can to detain him at home and to keep him interested exclusively in her. She is not entirely successful at first; then, just as she appears to have made him forget the world outside, her happiness is shattered, this time for good, by the insistent knocking of Captain Brennan, who brings orders from James Connolly, head of the Citizen Army, that Jack who, to his surprise, is spoken of as a Commandant, is to lead a reconnaissance attack on Dublin Castle. When it transpires that Nora has burned the letter containing the information that Jack was promoted Commandant two weeks before, he is furious. A primary conflict in the play, that between Jack's love for Nora on the one hand, and his devotion to a political cause on the other, is starkly presented by Nora: 'Is General Connolly an' th' Citizen Army goin' to be your only care? Is your home goin' to be only a place to rest in?' (lines 889-91). Jack does not appear to have much trouble in resolving this conflict. As the following piece of dialogue suggests, the cause of the Citizen Army takes precedence for him over the most precious human relationships. The 'nonsense' he refers to is his domestic life:

> **Nora** (*running over to him, and pleadingly putting her arms around him*). Jack, please, Jack, don't go out to-night an' I'll tell you; I'll explain everything.... send him away, an' stay with your little red-lipp'd Nora.
> **Clitheroe** (*removing her arms from around him*). None o' this nonsense, now; I want to know what you did with th' letter?

Following Jack's departure, O'Casey gives us a pathetic
interlude designed to reveal the appalling condition of the
mass of Dublin's poor in the early decades of the century.
Mollser is his representation of the diseased and long-suffering
slum-dwellers who formed a large proportion of the city's
population in 1916. She is in the final stages of a fatal
consumption, or tuberculosis. Her speech to Nora is ironic in
more ways than one. As she expresses her envy of Nora's
health and her happy home, she does not realise that both of
these are soon to prove incredibly fragile. There is further
irony in Bessie's violent threats, couched in biblical language,
against those Irish people who refuse to fight against the
Germans, and turn their weapons against the English
occupation forces in Ireland: 'But yous'll not escape from
th'arrow that flieth be night or th'sickness that wasteth be
day.... An' ladyship an'all, as some o'them may be, they'll be
scattered abroad, like th'dust in th'darkness!' (lines 956-9). The
irony of this will be completed in as gruesome a fashion as even
Nora's dearest enemy could wish when she loses her husband,
her child, and her reason. Nora's loss, however is only one
strand of the irony involved in Bessie's prophecy. Bessie herself
will be struck down in random fashion by a stray bullet; she
now calls disasters down on the heads of those, like Nora, who
are identified with the anti-British cause, but when disaster
strikes for Nora, it is Bessie who will prove her greatest
comfort.

The most notable feature of the first Act, indeed of the
play as a whole, is its highly-charged atmosphere. Strife and
conflict are endemic at every level: between Nora and Jack;
between The Covey and Peter; between Bessie and her
neighbours; between Irish nationalism and British imperialism;
between the British and German armies abroad. All of these
conflicts are expressed in emotionally charged, often violent,
language, featuring strong rhythms, colourful images and the
unremitting use of alliteration.

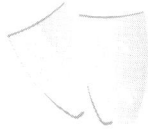

ACT 2

IRONIC CONTEMPLATION OF NATIONALISM

THIS Act is located in a public house, which is conveniently situated close to the scene of the great patriotic meeting frequently referred to in the previous Act. It is not difficult to imagine why this Act in particular should have been grossly offensive to Irish nationalists when the play was first produced in 1926. Ten years after the Easter Rising, those who had participated in it had achieved mythic status in the eyes of very many Irishmen and Irishwomen. Pádraig Pearse was widely regarded as a martyred hero, and the cause he and James Connolly had led the men of 1916 to fight and die for was revered as a noble one. In *The Plough and the Stars,* O'Casey has little time for the traditional nationalist pieties. The men who are to participate in the Rising are presented in this Act not always directly, but mainly through the satirical comments of Rosie Redmond, a prostitute. From her mercenary perspective (she will agree with any point of view that she thinks will please her clients), even these noble heroes are made to appear faintly ridiculous in their single-minded, mystical devotion to a cause: 'They're all in a holy mood... Th'solemn-looking dials on the whole o'them an' they marchin' to th' meetin'. You'd think they were th' glorious company of th' saints' (lines 32-5).

O'Casey achieves his most startling effect in this Act through the introduction of the silhouetted figure of a tall man speaking to the crowd at the meeting. The words this man speaks are the actual words of Pearse, but the context in which they are spoken exposes them to ironic contemplation, if not to ridicule. The Pearse-figure calls on his listeners to join him in a ritual blood-sacrifice for the freedom of Ireland, and glorifies such a course of action ('Bloodshed is a cleansing and sanctifying thing, and the nation that regards it as the final horror has lost its manhood', lines 58-60). The only visible

effect of these utterances is to arouse in Peter and Fluther
patriotic emotions which can only be assuaged by alcohol,
which in turn causes them to rant 'with the fulness of
emotional passion'. We know that Peter and Fluther are not
likely to respond to the call of the silhouetted orator to shed
their blood for the redemption of Ireland. Their actual response
is mock-heroic ('The blood was boilin' in me veins!.... I was
burnin' to dhraw me sword an' wave an' wave it over me', lines
111-18). It is difficult to take seriously the militant rhetoric of
the speaker, framed as it is by such comments, just as it is
difficult to take seriously The Covey's Marxist pronouncements
about the 'conthrol o' th' means o' production, rates of exchange
an' th' means of disthribution', addressed as they are in a
public house to the totally apolitical Rosie Redmond. The
atmosphere she creates makes any serious ideas appear totally
incongrous. It is left to Mrs. Gogan to expose further the hollow
pretensions of armchair patriots such as Peter, as she imagines
him and the other Foresters in their colourful uniforms
'hangin', at th' end of a rope, your eyes bulgin' an' your legs
twistin' an' jerkin', gaspin' an' gaspin' for breath while yous'
are thryin' to die for Ireland! '

When the voice of the silhouetted speaker celebrates once
more the virtues of war and heroism, his sentiments are
immediately undercut first by The Covey's retort that the only
war worth waging is for the economic emancipation of the
proletariat (lines 344-6) and then by an extended squabble
between two intoxicated women, Mrs. Gogan and Bessie
Burgess, about their claims to respectability. Bessie and Mrs.
Gogan first take issue over the non-participation of some young
Irishmen in the European war, but the discussion quickly
degenerates into the crudest personal abuse. Mrs. Gogan is
accused by Bessie of accepting charity under false pretences,
consorting with men in the public house, and perhaps having
children out of wedlock (lines 371-3). Bessie is accused in turn
of some unspecified nocturnal misdemeanours ('th sins of a
night's diversion', lines 387-8). Only the intervention of the
barman prevents physical violence between the contending
parties.

The patriotic speaker outside in the street has been emphasising the holiness of war. Inside the public house this sentiment is being parodied in the verbal battles of the intoxicated customers, and in their unsuccessful attempts to engage in physical conflict. The entire episode is farcical in its reliance on verbal abuse, mock battles and such stage business as the passing around of Mrs. Gogan's baby. Its main effect is to make all the serious issues raised by the play — patriotism, war, socialism — appear unreal and unimportant. The Covey's attempt to expose Fluther's inadequacy as an authority on the Labour movement is typical of what happens in this scene:

> **The Covey** (*emphatically*). Well, let us put it to th' test, then, an' see what you know about th' Labour movement: what's the mechanism of exchange?
> **Fluther** (*roaring, because he feels he is beaten*). How th' hell do I know what it is? There's nothin' about that in th' rules of our Thrades Union!
> **Barman** (*protestingly*). For God's sake, thry to speak easy, Fluther.
> **The Covey**. What does Karl Marx say about th' Relation of Value to th' Cost o' Production?
> **Fluther** (*angrily*). What th' hell do I care what he says? I'm Irishman enough not to lose me head be follyin' foreigners!
>
> (lines 524-35)

INCONGRUOUS EFFECTS

The emphasis here is not on issues but on personalities. The best man is not the one with the greatest knowledge, intelligence or even strength, but the one with the most effective line in verbal abuse and bluster. The style degenerates into cornerboy *cliché* ('Come on, come on, you lowser.... Here, out you go, me little bowsey.' lines 594-601). This part of Act Two is full of incongruous effects. The besotted Fluther assumes a ridiculously chivalrous pose as he defends Rosie against The Covey's reprimands ('Any lady that's in th' company of Fluther is goin' to get a fair hunt', lines 563-4). The two working-class comrades abuse each other in most uncomradely terms. Fluther, earlier intoxicated by patriotic sentiments, now forgets these as he turns his amorous attentions to Rosie.

The final episode of Act Two is heavy with irony. Commandant Jack Clitheroe and two of his fellow-patriots, Captain Brennan of the Citizen Army and Lieutenant Langon of the Irish Volunteers, have, as the stage-direction puts it, been 'mesmerized by the fervency of the speeches'. In their patriotic fervour, they renounce all human ties in favour of the cause of Ireland:

> **Capt. Brennan**. We won't have long to wait now.
> **Lieut. Langon**. Th' time is rotten ripe for revolution.
> **Clitheroe** (*to* **Lieut. Langon**). You have a mother, Langon.
> **Lieut. Langon**. Ireland is greater than a mother.
> **Capt. Brennan** (*to* **Clitheroe**). You have a wife, Clitheroe.
> **Clitheroe**. Ireland is greater than a wife.
>
> (lines 647-52)

ACT 3

THE REALITY OF POVERTY AS A BACKGROUND TO IDEALISM

THIS Act is located in the streets outside the tenement building which houses the Clitheroes, Mrs. Gogan, Bessie, Fluther and the rest. It is Easter Week 1916, and Jack Clitheroe is taking part in the Rising.

It is significant that O'Casey opens the Act, not with an episode involving military action, but with the dying Mollser and her mother Mrs. Gogan. The latter is vainly trying to detect some signs of improvement in her daughter's hopeless condition. O'Casey's purpose here is to dramatise the human suffering engendered by the deplorable living conditions in the Dublin slums of the early twentieth century. The episode makes a further point. While the men of 1916 are fighting for an ideal, people like Mollser are dying of neglect born of poverty. O'Casey does not present the Rising of 1916 as a struggle for a better way of life for the poor. He uses The Covey to express the idea that the Rising is not an adequate response to the sufferings endured by the Dublin working-classes. 'If they were fighting for any thin' worth while', The Covey says of the patriots, 'I wouldn' mind' (lines 194-5).

A larger theme of this Act, and of the play as a whole, is that while men theorise about socialism, nationalism and their visions of Ireland's destiny, and some of them fight and die for their dreams, women such as Nora Clitheroe suffer the anguish of separation and bereavement, and find the price of their loved ones' patriotism too high. The frightened, bewildered Nora goes in search of her husband at the barricades in a futile effort to save him for herself. As David Krause remarks, O'Casey desecrated the household gods of Ireland in *The Plough and the Stars* 'by identifying his Cathleen Ní Houlihan with the ragged women of the Dublin tenements, with Nora Clitheroe and Jinnie Gogan and Bessie Burgess, instead of with the 1916 martyrs. This did not mean that he was against the revolution and the martyrs; it meant that he was for the forgotten mothers and the wives. In the ironic context of the play, Ireland is no greater than her mothers and wives, for whom bloodshed has indeed become the final horror'. Jack Clitheroe's heroism has no positive, redemptive effect on Nora; all it achieves is the tragic absurdity of her collapse into hysteria, followed by the loss of her baby and ultimately by her insanity.

This Act is notable for some subtle and surprising insights into human nature involving O'Casey's anti-heroes and clowns: Bessie Burgess and Fluther Good in particular. In the previous Act, Fluther appeared to be a most unpromising candidate for heroism. The intervention of the barman was needed to save him from the embarrassment of having to fulfil his empty threats to fight The Covey. In this Act, we learn that even Fluther is capable of exemplary courage when called upon to display it. Mrs. Gogan talks of 'that madman, Fluther, running about through the night lookin' for Nora Clitheroe to bring her back when he heard she'd gone to folly her husband' (lines 48-51). In this exploit, Fluther exposes himself to real danger. Such is the excitement generated by the Rising that even The Covey and Peter forget their enmity as they join in describing the scenes of bloodshed they have witnessed in the streets. Bessie Burgess has undergone a transformation also. She is the same loud-mouthed, aggressive, violent critic of her neighbours and their ways, but a new side to her character emerges in an important stage-direction. As Mrs. Gogan helps Nora in her distress, Bessie 'gives a mug of milk to Mollser, silently'.

There is further emphasis on Nora's role as the chief suffering victim of her husband's patriotic endeavour. She has to endure not only an intense anxiety for Jack's welfare, but also the scorn of those involved in the Rising, who consider her behaviour cowardly and unworthy of her husband. All she can do by way of response is to curse the Volunteers for bringing about the Rising. It is noteworthy that the Rising is presented by O'Casey not mainly in terms of the heroic endeavours of the Irish Volunteers and the members of the Citizen Army, but as an affair involving fearful suffering, slaughter and chaos. Nora paints a vivid picture of the fear on the faces of the combatants as they refuse to look on the broken body of a mortally wounded man, 'a horrible tangled heap' (line 211). Nora's verdict on the significance of the Rising is absolutely true to her experience however others may judge it: 'They have dhriven away th' little happiness life had to spare for me' (lines 236-6).

COMIC REALITIES

In the midst of death there is life, and O'Casey balances his tragic realities with some notable comic ones. Fluther has had enough of the dangers of battle for the moment, and he now proposes a game of pitch-and-toss with The Covey. This is played to the accompaniment of the distant boom of a big artillery piece. Meanwhile, Bessie has discovered a new diversion. She returns from a shop-looting expedition bearing some valuable items, and this inspires Fluther to loot a public house. The episode involving the fashionably-dressed middle-class woman gives O'Casey an opportunity to indulge in a fairly obvious and not very successful caricature of a Dublin middle-class accent. The weakness of the portrait of this woman makes the vividness of the working-class characters all the more striking. (For an explanation of its inclusion in the play, see *Critical Comment. No. 15.*)

Bessie and Mrs. Gogan, never the best of friends, now begin to find much in common as they prepare to go looting shops together. Mrs. Gogan wonders how Bessie can reconcile her hymn-singing and high moral standards with her present activity. Bessie's conscience remains untroubled: she is not stealing but gathering up odds and ends misplaced 'in th' loose confusion of a general plundher!' (line 435). When they return from their looting their common pride in what they have acquired transforms their relationship. Mrs. Gogan is so enthralled by the loot that she is temporarily uninterested in the critical condition of her daughter Mollser (lines 503-5).

With the entry of Captain Brennan and Jack Clitheroe bearing the mortally-wounded Langon, O'Casey is again presenting the 1916 Rising in terms of its suffering and slaughter, its horror rather than its glory. Langon's face, as the stage-direction emphasises, is 'ghastly white' and 'momentarily convulsed with spasms of agony'. The most notable passage in this episode is the exchange between Jack Clitheroe and Captain Brennan:

> **Capt. Brennan** (*back to Clitheroe*). Why did you fire over their heads? Why didn't you fire to kill?
> **Clitheroe**. No, no, Bill; bad as they are, they're Irish men an' women.
> (**Brennan** *gently lets* LANGON *recline on the steps of the house indicated to the extreme* R., *holding him by an arm:* CLITHEROE *is* C., *watching* LANGON.)
> **Capt. Brennan** (*savagely*). Irish be damned! Attackin' an' mobbin' th' men that are riskin' their lives for them. If these slum lice gather at our heels again, plug one o' them, or I'll soon shock them with a shot or two meself!
>
> (lines 525-32)

Captain Brennan, we have to remind ourselves, is an officer in the Irish Citizen Army, founded by James Larkin and other champions of the oppressed to defend working people from attack. O'Casey, by dramatising Brennan's contempt for 'these slum lice' from among whom Clitheroe has sprung, is justifying his own rejection of the altered role of the Citizen Army as it allied itself in battle in 1916 with the mainly middle-class Irish Volunteers. (See the section headed *The Plough and the Stars and Irish Nationalism.*)

DIVIDED LOYALTIES

The reunion between Jack and Nora is all the more poignant because it is so short and final. Clitheroe is now torn by divided loyalties. He wants to stay with Nora, but his duty as a soldier, and as a human being, demands that he get help for the wounded Langon. He cannot now betray his comrades in arms. Nora has little or no sense of her husband's dilemma. Her pathetic attempts to keep him with her threaten to make a mockery of his heroism, and to destroy whatever respect his military activities have won for him from his comrades. His self-esteem combined with moral pressure from Captain Brennan finally overcome the force of Nora's pleadings, and he is forced to fling her from him. As the distracted Nora lies on the street, Bessie Burgess again performs an unexpected act of kindness as she lifts her in her arms and carries her into the house. Nora's shock has induced premature labour, and Bessie is determined to find a doctor. This emergency is juxtaposed with Fluther's drunken singing. Bessie now achieves her finest moment in the play so far. In spite of rifle and machine-gun fire, she 'firmly and swiftly' goes out to seek help for Nora, invoking divine protection as she does so. Her final prayer ('an' shelter me safely in th' shadow of thy wings') is cruelly ironic, since it is soon to be answered in her accidental and apparently meaningless death.

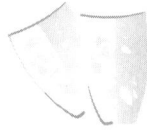

ACT 4

THE DARKNESS OF ADVERSITY

THIS Act is more sombre in tone than the first three. The stage-directions ensure that the setting matches the pitiless progress of the action. Bessie's attic room, for example, has 'a look of compressed confinement'. There is no light in the room except that provided by two candles and the fire. A coffin containing two bodies stands on two kitchen chairs.

The single concession to normality is the card game played by the men. From Fluther we learn that both Mollser and Nora's still-born child are lying in the same coffin. Common adversity has moderated the quarrelsome temperaments of the residents of the tenement. The Covey, instead of mouthing his tiresome Marxist slogans, now evokes pity for the dead Mollser, victim of hereditary tuberculosis which killed her father when she was a baby and forced her mother to look for work. Nora will never be the same following the death of her baby. Fluther and The Covey are at one in recognising Bessie's sterling qualities of character, her endurance and self-sacrifice.

The mood of the play is further darkened by the entry of Captain Brennan to announce the death of Jack Clitheroe. The most painful part of Brennan's account is not his description of Clitheroe's death, but his utterly empty words of hope, which assume darkly ironic overtones in the light of Nora's actual condition:

> **Capt. Brennan** (*defensively*). I took me chance as well as him.... He took it like a man. His last whisper was to "Tell Nora to be brave; that I'm ready to meet my God, an' that I'm proud to die for Ireland." An' when our General heard it he said that "Commandant Clitheroe's end was a gleam of glory." Mrs. Clitheroe's grief will be a joy when she realizes that she has had a hero for a husband.
>
> (lines 160-66)

At this stage in Nora's experience, such a notion as Jack's heroism is totally meaningless. She has made it clear throughout that she would infinitely prefer a living, unheroic husband to share her home than to be left to mourn a heroic dead one. His sacrifice has cost her both her sanity and her child. In O'Casey's vision of things this is what nationalistic politics have done to a representative family unit.

The closing moments of the play are fraught with ironies, not the least of which is the manner of Bessie's death. Throughout the play, she has been protesting her loyalty to the British connection. Shortly before her death she makes a firm declaration of her attachment to all things British, and her abomination of Irish Nationalism:

> **Corporal Stoddart**. All men in the district 'as to be rounded up. Somebody's giving 'elp to the snipers, an' we 'as to tike precautions. If I 'ad my wy I'd mike 'em all join up an' do their bit! But I suppose they an' you are all Shinners.
>
> **Blessie** (*who has been sinking into sleep, waking up to a sleepy vehemence*). Bessie Burgess is no Shinner, an' never had no thruck with anything spotted be th' fingers o' th' Fenians. But always made it her business to harness herself for Church whenever she knew that God Save The King was goin' to be sung at t'end of th' service: whose only son went to th' front in th' first contingent of the Dublin Fusiliers, an' that's on his way home carryin' a shatthered arm that he got fightin' for his King an' counthry!
>
> (lines 386-400)

Given her unflinching loyalty to King and Country, it is the cruellest of ironies that she should die from wounds inflicted by a British soldier.

LIGHT IN THE MIDST OF ADVERSITY

The events of the last Act are harrowing, but O'Casey does not end his play on a note of despair. We are made to feel that the characters who remain will preserve their lives and their buoyancy of spirit in a dangerous world. They are born survivors. Their sense of the ludicrous, the eccentric and the absurd serves them well as a defence against the harsher realities of life. Human touches abound everywhere in the closing moments of Act Four, and in spite of some melo-dramatic touches O'Casey preserves a rare truth to life. Bessie's speech just after she has been shot is a good example of this. She has been showing nobler and finer feelings for others, particularly for the distracted Nora, in the second half of the play, but O'Casey preserves her flawed humanity in this speech. He does not let her die the death of a noble, self-sacrificing heroine — a death which would be false to her nature. The words he gives her are a perfect expression of her vehement, earthy character:

> **Bessie** (*with an arrested scream of fear and pain*).
> 'Merciful God, I'm shot, I'm shot, I'm shot! Th' life's
> pourin' out o'me! (*To Nora*) I've got this through . . .
> through you. . . through you, you bitch, you! . . . O
> God, have mercy on me! . . . (To Nora) You wouldn't
> stop quiet, no, you wouldn't, you wouldn't, blast
> you! Look at what I'm afther gettin', look at what
> I'm afther gettin' . . .

> (lines 579-85)

IRONIC EFFECTS

O'Casey achieves some other notably ironic effects in Act Four. Given his rejection of religious belief, it is difficult not to find ironic intent in his choice of the hymn 'I do believe, I will believe/That Jesus died for me' for Bessie to sing as she dies. There are other ironies associated with O'Casey's choice of musical items in the last Act. Some commentators have found it shocking that Nora should be led away in her distraction of mind, having been deprived of the light of reason, 'to the strains of Newman's great hymn, 'Lead kindly light, amid th' encircling gloom'. The irony of Bessie's choice of hymn is completed as she herself is dying ('Jesus Christ, me sight's goin'! It's all dark, dark! Nora, hold me hand!') Bessie is not merely deprived of the light she has earlier invoked; she is also deprived of the comfort of Nora's help at the end of her life. Her only request in the course of the play, her dying one, cannot be met by Nora.

Even more remarkable is the fact that the final emotion of the play should be expressed in a rendering of the propagandist war song, 'Keep the home fires burning'. There are various layers of irony in this. As Tinley and Stoddart sing, it is the city of Dublin that is burning, not its home fires. The song is sung in the living-room of Bessie, who has just been killed by those who are singing it. The theme of the song suggests its own ironies. It encourages the loved ones of the soldiers at the front to be of good heart until 'the boys come home'. Bessie, the only character in the play who has a son on active service with the British Army, is an ironic victim of the same army whose cause she has consistently championed. The song cruelly mocks her faith and endurance and underlines the fact that no home fires will burn when her son returns from the war.

The Characters

NORA CLITHEROE

NORA, THE VICTIM OF OUTSIDE FORCES

NORA is the chief character of the play. Everything that happens inside and outside her tenement dwelling turns directly or indirectly on her. Most of the activities of the other characters are significant insofar as they affect her. She is primarily the suffering victim of forces outside her control, the wife whose husband chooses to leave her to serve a patriotic cause, wanting only to be mistress of a good and happy home, and being denied even this limited happiness, finding herself caught up in the anarchy and destructiveness of war and losing everything that matters to her in the process. In the scheme of *The Plough and the Stars*, she is the chief representative of humanitarian sentiment. It is mainly through the medium of Nora that O'Casey reflects the brutality of war and exposes the inadequacies of the sentimental, self-glorifying patriotism exemplified in the military figures of the play, who include her husband Jack.

Her earliest appearances suggest a strength of character and a firmness of purpose which events will later modify. The emphasis in the opening movement of the play is on her anxiety to rise above her humble station, and to make a home free from the intrusion of neighbours such as Bessie Burgess. The lock which Fluther fixes on her door is a step in this direction. Mrs. Gogan is somewhat offended at her 'notions of upperosity', suggested by her purchase of an expensive hat, and her possession of a silver fox fur. Offence is also caused to her neighbours by her insistence on observing the polite conventions, and her unwillingness to continue living in a tenement house. She exercises a rigid control over the domestic behaviour of The Covey and Uncle Peter. She is introduced as a sprightly, strong-minded girl with distinct ambitions for self-improvement. When Peter and The Covey engage in one of their tiresome bouts of animosity, she accuses them of tearing down the 'little bit of respectability that a body's trying to build'.

FRAGILE HAPPINESS

Early in Act One, we are given an ominous hint that Nora's domestic happiness, the anchor of her life, is somewhat fragile. Mrs. Gogan, who never misses a detail, has observed that Jack's ardour for Nora has cooled, and that she must resort to dressing herself rather ostentatiously in order to keep him interested in her. For the remainder of the play, keeping Jack with her is her single preoccupation For this reason the portrayal of Nora is severely restricted, and its interest limited. She is a representative type rather than a fully realised individual. With the entry of Jack it becomes obvious that she is not as strong-willed as she appeared earlier. She is obviously unsure of her husband's exclusive devotion to her, which is what she demands: she rightly senses that he has given up his active involvement in the Citizen Army not because of her, but because of his supposed lack of promotion in the body. As we are soon to learn, she does not want to put Jack's loyalty to the test. Jack has in fact been promoted, but she has destroyed the letter of promotion, rightly fearing that this honour would induce him to give all his time to the national cause. Her well-meant deception is a serious mistake from her point of view. When Captain Brennan arrives with mobilisation orders from James Connolly, and reveals the news of Jack's promotion, the latter has no hesitation in putting his public activity before his wife's happiness, and Nora is bitterly humiliated.

NORA'S MISCALCULATIONS

Her attempts to achieve her single ambition — her exclusive right to her husband's time and attention — are fraught with errors and miscalculations. Her deception of Jack over his promotion is only the first of these. When the military action of the Rising is at its most intense, she follows him to bring him back, and makes an embarrassing scene at the barricades. Her intervention shows the extent to which her devotion to her husband causes her to ignore good sense and discretion. As Jack points out, his comrades will now believe that he sent her in order to have an excuse to abandon his post and see her safely home. She may well have turned all the risks he has taken 'into a laugh', as he puts it. Her possessive love for Jack blinds her to his very real dilemma. He now has to contend with a conflict within himself between his desire to remain with her and the demands of his army role. Back in the tenement with Nora, he wishes he had never left with her, but for him it is now a question of giving in to Nora or being untrue to his comrades and abandoning the mortally-wounded Langon.

Nora's view of Jack's situation is distressingly simple-minded: 'I want you to be true to me, Jack . . . I'm your dearest comrade.' It also appears callous in the circumstances, since, as she is imploring Jack to stay with her, the dying Langon is calling out for help. At this point, whatever may have been the dramatist's intentions, it is impossible not to have sympathy for her husband's predicament. He could only lose respect and stature if he submitted to Nora's entreaties to stay.

In the last Act, Nora is deprived of her reason. For all her early strength of mind, she has proved unable to face the shock of rejection. In O'Casey's scheme, the psychological implications of her plight hardly matter. What is important is her representative status as chief victim of the horrors of war, and of what the dramatist sees as the misguided idealism of the participants in the national struggle.

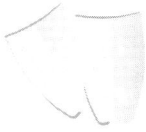

JACK CLITHEROE

JACK, A CONDITIONAL DEDICATION TO THE CAUSE

IN drama, as in other kinds of imaginative literature, our first impressions of the characters are always significant. Jack Clitheroe does not get a particularly favourable introduction. O'Casey's stage direction suggests a weak character: 'His face has none of the strength of Nora's. It is a face in which is the desire for authority, but without the power to attain it.'

Clitheroe is not a heroic figure. It becomes clear as the action proceeds that his dedication to the national cause is, at best, a conditional one. He has, as Nora observes, given up the Citizen Army out of pique at not being made a Captain. Mrs. Gogan confirms this. When he harboured his ambitions of advancement, she remarks, he bought a Sam Brown belt which he delighted in showing off to his neighbours. If we are to trust her report, Jack regards the Citizen Army as a means of indulging his vanity and love of self-display. On the principle that we tend to attribute our own worst motives and sentiments to others, Mrs. Gogan may not be far wrong. Jack envies Brennan now that the latter has been promoted Captain, and thinks that the night parade is the 'first chance Brennan has of showing himself off since they made a Captain of him.'

It is certainly significant that Jack rejoins the Citizen Army immediately he gets word of his promotion to Commandant and is given command of a battalion. It is also significant that he deals harshly with Nora when he discovers that she has withheld news of his promotion from him. By making Jack a representative figure in the Citizen Army, O'Casey is indicating his disapproval of the direction that body had taken in 1916.

In the conflict between the values represented by Nora and those embodied in Jack, O'Casey directs our sympathies mainly in her favour, particularly in the early part of the play. The weight of emphasis is overwhelmingly on *her* suffering and distress, which are due in the main to his decisions. We are made familiar with her preoccupations and her motivation, which are seen as important in themselves. His thoughts and actions, on the other hand, are important mainly as they concern her, and as they impinge on her welfare and happiness.

CLITHEROE, HIS DEATH AN IRONIC COMMENT

In the second half of the play, particularly after Jack has become involved in the military operations of the Citizen Army, he becomes a somewhat more sympathetic figure than he appeared to be in the first half. Whatever his motives for rejoining the Army, he takes part in the fighting and meets his death in action. Captain Brennan's account of his death invests him with heroic dignity, although it must be remembered that such accounts as Brennan's are to be treated with caution. He and Brennan, we are told, fought till their post was in flames; Clitheroe's last words are of his pride in dying for Ireland, and James Connolly is quoted as having described his end as 'a gleam of glory'. We should, however, interpret Brennan's words not as evidence of a desire on O'Casey's part to make us think better of Jack at the end than we did at the beginning, but as an ironic comment on the value of heroism and military glory. O'Casey's ironic intention is clear from the context in which Brennan's laudatory words are spoken. When he tells Bessie that 'Mrs. Clitheroe's grief will be joy when she realises that she has had a hero for a husband', his words have an embarrassingly hollow ring, since at this stage his heroism has rendered Nora incapable of any kind of sensible response: she is beyond being able to feel either grief or joy.

Jack's personal qualities, his early vanity, his love of display, his later sense of duty and loyalty to his wounded comrade, his fighting spirit, are less significant than his representative role. He stands for the principle he himself enunciates in the public house before the Rising, 'Ireland is greater than a wife'. The play shows how this principle works out in practice for his wife and for himself. In the end, he is as much the victim of his own delusions as Nora is.

FLUTHER GOOD

FLUTHER, LIFE AND HOPE

FLUTHER represents the most subtle piece of characterisation in the play. He is its outstanding comic figure, a superb fool, full of splendid contradictions, capable of endless surprises, endowed with an impressive turn of phrase, resilient, witty, humorous, resourceful, and always entertaining. He is the character who breathes life and hope into a play whose atmosphere would otherwise be oppressively gloomy.

In the early episodes he acts the part of the stage-clown with energy and spirit. He also looks the part, with the few tufts of reddish hair over his ears, his scrubby red moustache, his seedy black suit, black bow tie and faded jerry hat. He is an inveterate tippler, but means to conquer the habit before he dies. We know he will never quite get around to fulfilling this resolution. He is liable to worry about his health. When the lugubrious Mrs. Gogan, whose great topic of conversation is death, remarks on Fluther's cough and enlarges on its fatal possibilities, his good spirits momentarily give way to morbid fears ('I feel as dizzy as bedamned. I hope I didn't give up the beer too suddenly'). He soon recovers his equilibrium, however, and assumes one of his other roles, that of the play's homespun philosopher, when The Covey mentions religion in connection with politics. This gives Fluther an opening for one of his most profound and penetrating witticisms: 'There's no need to bring religion into it. I think we ought to have as great a regard for religion as we can, so as to keep it out of as many things as possible.'

PATRIOTIC FANTASIES

In Act Two, in the bar, Fluther emerges in yet another role, that of Irish patriot. The rhetoric of the meeting has worked on his emotions to the extent that he imagines himself taking part in the fight for Irish freedom. The same patriotic fervour has induced in him a strong desire for alcohol, which in turn strengthens both his eloquence and his patriotic fantasies: 'You can die now, Fluther, for you've seen the shadow-dhreams of the past leppin' to life in the bodies of livin' men that show, if we were without a titther o' courage for centuries, we're vice-versa now!' This rhetorical outburst and others like it do not indicate that Fluther will ever actually fight for Ireland; he prefers mock-heroic battles to real ones. Under provocation from The Covey, who has no time for nationalist rhetoric, Fluther's sentimental patriotism intensifies: he remembers his mother's injunction to him in infancy to be faithful to 'the Shan Van Vok'. He now becomes the military braggart, the *miles gloriosus* of traditional comedy, proudly displaying wounds he claims, or imagines, were inflicted by a 'sabre slice' from a dragoon in O'Connell Street and 'a skelp from a bobby's baton' at a Labour meeting. It is a short step from this self-enhancement to his next role, that of chivalrous, quixotic defender of the honour of Rosie Redmond, who has been insulted by The Covey. This defence of Rosie is conducted verbally: Fluther is saved from the necessity of physical combat with The Covey by the timely intervention of the barman. With a characteristic flight of fancy, Fluther interprets this encounter as a victory for himself, and this stimulates him to provide Rosie with exaggerated impressions of his physical prowess ('I hit a man last week, Rosie, an' he's fallin' yet'). The apparently wide gulf between Fluther's heroic conception of himself and what we have seen of the real man in action is a fertile source of comedy.

FLUTHER'S CONTRADICTORY NATURE

To describe Fluther simply as a clown, a braggart and a comic buffoon is, however, to leave out at least half the truth about him. Act Three provides us with new and surprising insights to his character. The man who appeared so worried about his health and whose desire for physical combat appeared so suspect earlier now risks his life to rescue Nora Clitheroe and bring her back safely from the scene of battle. This time he does not boast of his brave achievement, because it is a real one for a change. Indeed, when Nora draws attention to his courage ('I'd have been lyin' in the streets only for him'), he makes no comment but proposes a game of pitch-and-toss. O'Casey, however, even at this point in the play, clearly does not wish to present Fluther as the strong, silent hero. He has taken a considerable personal risk to save Nora; he now takes the same kind of risk to loot a public house so that he can become blind drunk. The presentation of Fluther is attended by many contradictions of this kind. Having defended the honour of Rosie, he goes off with her to enjoy her favours; having made the firmest of resolutions to abstain from drink in future, we see him drunk twice within a short time.

Fluther has some of his best moments in the last Act. He shows no fear of the British soldiers, and puts them in their place a few times with unexpected and devastating logic. When Corporal Stoddart declares that it is the duty of a man to fight for his country, Fluther's retort ('You're not fighting for your country here, are you?') is unanswered and, indeed, unanswerable. Again, when Sergeant Tinley complains that the Irish rebels are not fighting fair because they refuse to come into the open, Fluther is an inspiring apologist for his fellow-countrymen: 'Fight fair! A few hundhred scrawls o' chaps with a couple o' guns an' rosary beads, again a hundhred thousant men with horse, fut an' artillery. . . an' he wants us to fight fair . . . D'ye want us to come out in our skins an' throw stones?' The finest tribute to Fluther's sterling qualities of character comes from the bereaved Mrs. Gogan, even if the end of her speech appears unduly sentimental:

> **Mrs. Gogan** (*to* **Fluther**). I'll never forget what you done for me, Fluther, goin' around at th' risk of your life settlin' everything with th' undhertaker an' th' cemetery people. When all me own were afraid to put their noses out, you plunged like a good one through hummin' bullets, an' they knockin' fire out o' th' road, tinklin' through th' frightened windows, an' splashin' themselves to pieces on th' walls! An' you'll find, that Mollser in th' happy place she's gone to, won't forget to whisper, now an' again, th' name o' Fluther.

> (Act 4, lines 351-60)

One effect of this tribute is to suggest that the real heroes of the play are not those who have gone to war, but those who, like Fluther, have remained behind to perform humane services against frightening odds, without reward or recognition.

BESSIE BURGESS

POWERFUL AND IMPOSING

OUR earliest impressions of Bessie are far from favourable. She is the outsider in the tenement group, hostile to her neighbours, vehement in manner, bitter in tongue, sharply critical of almost everybody and everything around her, at odds with Nora in particular. She has the most powerful and imposing personality of all the characters in the play. She needs to be assertive and strong-minded, being at present alone in the world, professing the minority Protestant religion, and aggressively supporting the British connection against the various kinds of nationalist opinion current among her neighbours. Her very first appearance is the signal for a quarrel, and the descriptive stage-direction is far from reassuring: 'Her face is a dogged one, hardened by toil, and a little coarsened by drink. She looks scornfully and viciously at Nora'. She has two distinct kinds of speech. One is coarse, threatening and abusive ('You little over-dressed throllop you, for one pin I'd paste the white face o' you'). The other, by contrast, is stately and impressive, based on the Authorised Version of the Bible ('thryin' to speak proud things, an lookin' like a mighty one in the congregation o' th' people').

Bessie's main preoccupation throughout is with the cause of Britain in the Great War. She is proud of the fact that her son is serving in the trenches, and bitterly critical of those Irishmen and Irishwomen who do not lend support to the British war effort. She regards Jack Clitheroe and those who prefer the cause of Irish independence to that of the British Empire as traitors and parasites. As she watches the march past of the Dublin Fusiliers on their way to the Western Front, she expresses her pride in them and her contempt for Irish nationalists in splendid apocalyptic language which has a wonderfully sonorous ring and which conveys a self-satisfied threat of vengeance on all those who fail to do their duty to the British Empire. This utterance, and many others like it, make Bessie sound like an Old Testament prophetess with a Dublin accent:

> **Bessie** (*speaking in towards the room*). There's th' men marchin' out into th' dhread dimness o' danger, while th' lice is crawlin' about feedin' on th' fatness o' the land! But yous'll not escape from th' arrow that flieth be night, or th' sickness that wasteth be day.... An' ladyship an' all, as some o' them may be, they'll be scattered abroad, like th' dust in th' darkness!

> (Act 1, lines 953-9)

BESSIE'S THERAPEUTIC EFFECT

The tremendous rhetoric of vituperation in which Bessie indulges at the expense of her neighbours, who often reply with equal vehemence, does not necessarily imply total enmity, as later events make abundantly clear. The fluctuating relationship between Bessie and Mrs. Gogan illustrates this. In the public house scene in Act Two, these two women have what, on the face of it, appears like an irreconcilable quarrel. Bessie imputes unspecified forms of moral turpitude to Mrs. Gogan, who in turn stresses her adversary's drunkenness. This exchange is followed by suggestions of accepting charity under false pretences, bearing children out of wedlock, and other lapses from virtue. Another quarrel in Act Three is quickly followed by a happy reconciliation between Bessie and Mrs. Gogan as, united in a plundering expedition, they exchange delighted comments on the items they have looted. We now realise that their quarrels are less occasions for estrangement than opportunities for vigorous social contact; they are largely ritual exercises which clear the air, relieve tension and boredom and thus have a therapeutic effect on those condemned to the claustrophobic existence of tenement life. Bessie's abusive outbursts are thus not to be taken entirely at face value.

The vindictive side to Bessie's character is apparent in Act Three, where she revels in the suffering inflicted by the British forces on the Irish insurrectionists. From her window she taunts Jack, Nora and Captain Brennan as Lieutenant Langon lies mortally wounded. Even her cruel jibes, however, are shot through with earthy humour at Captain Brennan's expense. She has a highly-developed sense of the absurd and the ludicrous: 'An' th' professor of chicken-butcherin' there, finds he's up against somethin' a little tougher even than his own chickens, an' that's sayin' a lot'.

COURAGE AND A SENSE OF KINSHIP

Bessie, like Fluther, is a character full of surprises. These emerge in the latter half of the play. Her fierce, defensive rhetoric conceals a good heart, stubborn courage and a real sense of kinship with her neighbours. Whatever earlier appearances may have suggested, Bessie does have a kindly nature. She can pass Nora and Mrs. Gogan with her head in the air, but then quietly and unobtrusively give a mug of milk to Mrs. Gogan's ailing daughter. When Nora becomes dangerously ill, Bessie's fundamental goodness of heart, courage and unselfishness are made apparent in her journey in search of a doctor through streets echoing to the sound of gunfire. When Nora needs constant attention, it is Bessie who provides it, keeping a sleepless and exhausting vigil by her bedside, and protecting her rest from intrusion. She dies to save Nora from being shot at the window. This last gesture transforms her into the real heroine of a play in which various spurious and ironically observed forms of heroism loom so large.

Bella – War
Fighting

Like Fluther, Bessie is a paradoxical character. She is alternately belligerent and gentle, ferocious in manner and kind of heart, prepared to risk her life for the wife of the sworn enemy of the cause she so ardently believes in. She takes a high moral stand on most issues, and is much given to self-righteous pronouncements and vindications of the probity of her own character and ways, yet she can see no real contradiction between this and her participation in a looting expedition which deprives helpless traders of valuable property. Even her great heroic gesture in saving Nora's life is surrounded by ambiguity. She curses Nora for having caused her death ('You wouldn't stop quiet, no, you wouldn't, you wouldn't, blast you!'). Her dying moments are filled with fervent prayers, pleas for help from the ineffectual Nora and curses on the latter for not responding. Her end is altogether appropriate in the light of the flawed, exuberant manner of her life.

Other Characters

MRS. GOGAN

MRS. Gogan is not a major character, although she has more lines to speak than any of the others. Her life has been, and is throughout the action of the play, fraught with anxiety, sadness, and the fear of the imminent death of her daughter Mollser, who has an incurable disease. Her marital experiences have made Mrs. Gogan familiar with the experience of bereavement. Her husband has died of tuberculosis, and Mrs. Gogan is constantly preoccupied with the thought of death. It is her great single theme. Her obsession with this subject is such that when Fluther coughs, she has visions of his demise. She is able to draw on her extensive acquaintance with case-histories to cite the example of an apparently healthy woman who died suddenly of a slight cold in her chest. When Fluther goes in search of Nora, Mrs. Gogan imagines him splashed all over with blood, ready to whisper his hasty final confession. Even her dreams are of Fluther's death. When years of imagining and anticipating death finally give way to its reality, and Mollser dies, Bessie thinks this must be a terrible blow to Mrs. Gogan. Fluther puts Bessie right on this subject: 'A terrible blow? Sure, she's in her element now, woman, mixin' earth to earth, an' ashes t' ashes an' dust to dust, an' revellin' in plumes an' hearses, last days an' judgements'. What Fluther means is that Mollser's death has now given Mrs. Gogan, a greater right and opportunity than ever before to indulge in her favourite occupation and to extract the utmost satisfaction from it. O'Casey underlines the accuracy of Fluther's observation in a stage-direction. 'Mrs. Gogan comes in tearfully, and a little proud of the importance of being connected directly with death'. Mrs. Gogan's morbid preoccupation with death and all its trappings is perfectly comprehensible in psychological terms. Since she has been living in yearlong expectation of Mollser's death since her daughter's infancy, her greatest single means of defence against its ultimate arrival has been to cultivate it, to think and talk about it, and to expect it, so that when it comes it will be a familiar, and not a shocking thing. Now that it has come, being related to the dead gives Mrs. Gogan, who has never been the focus of much attention in her own right, a temporary centrality for which she yearns.

PETER FLYNN

PETER Flynn is a buffoon, and is seldom more than a figure of fun. He is not one of O'Casey's most interesting or successful pieces of characterisation. He totally lacks Fluther's humour, his humanity, his subtlety and his complexity. He undergoes no significant change or development in the course of the play, and his puerile conflicts with The Covey are nonsensical and tiresome. He behaves in an idiotic and childish way from beginning to end, and serves no really useful purpose either personally or dramatically. O'Casey uses Peter as a vehicle for satirising the political outlook he professes: the ineffectual nationalism which spends itself parading in ostentatious, antique uniforms, singing patriotic songs and looking to a romanticised, unreal past for its inspiration. At the personal level, it is difficult to have much respect for a man who can claim that he's 'so terrible dawny' that a fight leaves him 'weak for a long time afterwards', and who almost immediately tells The Covey that he will take his life violently.

THE COVEY, AN UNCONGENIAL MOUTHPIECE

The Covey has little enough to recommend him as a psychological study, and is one of the least attractive personalities in the play, if we exclude Peter. He is, however, important as a mouthpiece for some of O'Casey's own views on politics, society and religion. The puzzling thing here is why the dramatist chose so uncongenial a mouthpiece for his ideas as The Covey. He is longwinded, tiresome, tactless, humourless and colourless; he has little or no social grace, and his main talent is for irritating those around him with his unwelcome and unpopular ideas. He enjoys controversy, particularly when the topic is the condition of society; this gives him the opportunity to canvass his Marxist views in a graceless and unimaginative way. He is not the kind of man who could conceivably convert multitudes to Marxism. He is able to parrot some of its better-known ideas, but he is scarcely a persuasive exponent of socialist doctrine. Such is his blindness to human reality that he offers to let Rosie Redmond have a copy of his favourite Marxist tome. He can be sardonic and penetrating in his comments on the limitations of Fluther and Peter Flynn, and he exposes some of the shortcomings of doctrinaire nationalism. He fails to convince anybody, however, that international communism has anything better to offer. The Covey, like many of those who commit themselves to rigid, doctrinaire systems, is less interested in the welfare of individual human beings than in humanity in the abstract. He calls people 'comrade', but behaves towards them in a most uncomradely way, spending much of his time taunting Peter and quarrelling with Fluther. There is nothing humane about The Covey. Socialism implies a belief in the brotherhood of man. Ironically, it is those who understand nothing of socialist theory who put this belief into practice: Bessie and Fluther in particular.

The Plough and the Stars and Irish Nationalism

THE play is set against the background of the Easter Rising of 1916. It may be read as O'Casey's interpretation of the most critical event in modern Irish history. His presentation of the Rising and of its effects on the lives of the deprived tenement-dwellers who form the majority of his *dramatis personae* can best be understood in the light of his own experience of Irish political and social history in the years immediately preceding 1916. Of special importance here is his involvement with the Irish Citizen Army, and his disillusionment with its leadership and its policies.

The 1916 Rising was not a popular movement. At the time it took place, there was, as Eoin Mac Neill, the leader of the Irish Volunteers, pointed out, no widespread popular discontent with British rule. It was planned in secret by a small, unrepresentative group of Volunteers who were members of the IRB and who, early in 1916, took James Connolly, leader of the Citizen Army, into their confidence. The Citizen Army, founded by Jim Larkin in 1913 to protect striking workers from attack, was revived in 1914 largely on the initiative of O'Casey. It was strongly committed to socialist ideas, particularly to the public ownership of national resources; one of its primary aims was 'to sink all differences of birth, privilege and creed under the common name of the Irish people'. It stood for the achievement of equal rights and opportunities for all.

O'CASEY'S DISILLUSIONMENT WITH CONNOLLY

From the beginning of the Great War of 1914-18, Connolly had made up his mind that he would work for an insurrection in Ireland with a view to setting up a republic which would uphold the rights of the working-class. O'Casey's disillusionment with Connolly arose when he decided that the socialist leader had become a militant nationalist, and particularly when he observed that Connolly had entered into a cordial relationship with the more militant members of the Council of the Irish Volunteers. O'Casey supported the cause of international socialism, the main enemy of which, he believed, was the narrow nationalism he thought Connolly and the militants among the Irish Volunteers were now embracing. In *The Plough and the Stars,* The Covey puts O'Casey's point of view on this issue: 'Look here, comrade, there's no such thing as an Irishman, or an Englishman, or a German or a Turk; we're all only human bein's' (Act 1, lines 314-16).

In his small book, *The Story of the Irish Citizen Army,* O'Casey records the sense of betrayal he experienced as he observed Connolly's espousal of militant nationalism. 'It is difficult', O'Casey wrote, 'to understand the almost revolutionary change that was manifesting itself in Connolly's nature. The Labour movement seemed to be regarded by him as a decrescent force, while the essence of nationalism began to assume the finest elements of his nature. His articles that now appeared in the *Workers' Republic* with consistent regularity, the speeches that he delivered at various demonstrations and assemblies, all proclaimed that Jim Connolly had stepped from the narrow byway of Irish socialism on to the broad and crowded highway of Irish nationalism. The vision of the suffering world's humanity was shadowed by the nearer oppression of his own people, and in a few brief months, pressed into a hidden corner of his soul the accumulated thoughts of a lifetime, and opened his broad heart to ideas that altered the entire trend of his being. The high creed of Irish nationalism became his daily rosary, while the higher creed of international humanity that had so long bubbled from his eloquent lips was silent for ever, and Irish labour lost a leader.'

MERGING OF NATIONALIST AND SOCIALIST POLICIES

The truth was that Connolly had become, if anything, more militant and more nationalist in outlook than the more extreme members of the Military Council of the Volunteers who were planning an insurrection. In 1915, he organised drilling and training sessions for the Citizen Army. One battle exercise was arranged under the walls of Dublin Castle. O'Casey alludes to this in *The Plough and the Stars*: 'At two o'clock a.m. the army will leave Liberty Hall for a reconnaissance attack on Dublin Castle — Com. Gen. Connolly' (Act 1, lines 855-7). The Irish Volunteer militants who were planning their own insurrection realised that if Connolly proceeded with his own military uprising their plans would be in jeopardy, so they persuaded him early in 1916 to agree to act with them. He was sworn into the IRB and became a member of its Military Council. This, as O'Casey later pointed out, meant that the Citizen Army was becoming the militant left wing of the Irish Volunteers. O'Casey could not accept without protest the abandonment by the Citizen Army of the socialist identity, and its espousal of what he could only regard as a self-destructive, militant nationalism. In his eyes, this was bound to compromise the purity of its cause, which was that of a workers' republic. Connolly, on the other hand, mistakenly believed that an Irish insurrection would be the impetus for an international socialist revolution. In *The Plough and the Stars*, O'Casey allows The Covey to express his own opposition to the involvement of the Citizen Army in militant nationalist politics. The Covey argues that those who carry the Citizen Army flag, the Plough and the Stars, at a nationalist demonstration, are bringing disgrace on it 'because it's a Labour flag, an' was never meant for politics.... What does th' design of th' field plough, bearin' on it th' stars of th' heavenly plough mean, if it's not Communism? It's a flag that should only be used when we're buildin' th' barricades to fight for a Workers' Republic!' (Act 1, lines 649-54).

MISGIVINGS

O'Casey's misgivings about the motivation behind the 1916 Rising find expression in *The Plough and the Stars*. Some of the published views of Pádraig Pearse on the need to assert Irish national feeling through armed conflict with the forces of occupation are used in the play in contexts which make them sound incongruous or even faintly ridiculous. The Voice of the Speaker is heard enunciating Pearse's mystical glorification of military action and bloodshed as agents of a reviving national spirit: 'We must be ready to pour out the same red wine in the same glorious sacrifice, for without shedding of blood there is no redemption!' (Act 2, lines 127-30). As these stirring words are heard, most of the customers in the public house are indifferent to the Speaker's sentiments, concentrating instead on drinking and quarrelling over petty personal issues. The one thinking man among them, The Covey, describes the speaker's exaltation of war as 'Dope, dope', expressing the view that the only war worth waging is one for 'th' economic emancipation of th' proletariat' (Act 2, lines 344-6).

The edited words of Pearse thus have a very hollow ring in the context O'Casey prepares for them. It should be noted that the voice of the Speaker expresses the sentiments of Connolly as well as those of Pearse and the national question. Pearse, finding hope for the future in the bloodshed of the European War, declared that 'the old heart of the earth' needed to be warmed by the red wine of the battlefields. Connolly deplored the fact that so many Irishmen were fighting in France for the British Empire: their representatives in *The Plough and the Stars* are Bessie's son and the Dublin Fusiliers leaving for the front at the end of Act One. Connolly, like Pearse, felt strongly that a blood sacrifice on Irish soil was a necessary preliminary to national resurrection. 'No agency', Connolly declared, 'less powerful than the red tide of war on Irish soil will ever enable the Irish race to record its self-respect or to establish its national dignity. Without the slightest trace of irreverence, but with all due humility and awe, we recognise that of us, as of mankind before Calvary, it may truly be said, without the shedding of blood there is no redemption.'

THE PLIGHT OF CIVILIANS

Both the Citizen Army and the Irish Volunteers are represented in *The Plough and the Stars,* the former by Jack Clitheroe and Captain Brennan, the latter by Lieutenant Langon. O'Casey might have emphasised the unequal, heroic struggle of the small force of fewer than two thousand ill-equipped volunteers against thousands of British troops. It is true that there are a few scattered comments on the daring of those who took part in the Rising, notably from Fluther in response to the jibes of the British soldier (Act 4, lines 484-9). O'Casey's main focus, however, is on the suffering endured by the civilian victims of the fighting, particularly Nora and Bessie. If the play has a point to make about the Rising, it is surely that whatever sacrifice some of its heroes may have made, it was not on behalf of their wives and families, whose representative, Nora Clitheroe, is allowed to suffer beyond endurance. There is no suggestion that the Rising confers immediate or long-term benefit on O'Casey's group of tenement-dwellers. It is irrelevant to Mollser and to her mother; it is fatal to Jack Clitheroe and to Bessie; it leaves Nora a childless, insane widow; it appears a futile, meaningless exercise to The Covey; Fluther is drunk for much of its duration, while its significance for Peter Flynn is less than profound. It is noteworthy that the single positive thing about the struggle from the point of view of Bessie, Mrs. Gogan and Fluther is that it provides them with an opportunity to plunder shops; for them, this enlivens an otherwise ridiculous and dangerous existence.

As Hugh Hunt points out, Nora's outcry against her husband's participation in the Rising becomes a condemnation of the Rising itself. Fluther has earlier felt some patriotic stirrings, but as the Rising is nearing its climax, he drunkenly declares that 'the whole city can topple home to hell' for all he cares. It is also significant that O'Casey's treatment of his two representatives of the Citizen Army is less than adulatory. Brennan is seen by his colleague Jack Clitheroe as a vain, ostentatious figure with a love of display, while Clitheroe is seen by his neighbours in much the same light. Brennan's heroism is further undercut by the emphasis on his occupation as a chicken-butcher, in which capacity he is celebrated by Bessie for the toughness of his chickens. In *The Plough and the Stars*, O'Casey takes an ironic look at the conventionally heroic view of the Rising, a view which had become the established one by the time he wrote his play almost a decade after the event.

In *The Plough and the Stars*, O'Casey offers not merely a revisionist view of the 1916 Rising and its effects; the play also implies a rejection of political activity, which at best is made to appear futile and absurd, and at worst inimical to human welfare. Most of the political activity is focused on the meeting in Act Two. The tall man who addresses this meeting preaches the gospel of militant nationalism ('There are many things more horrible than bloodshed, and slavery is one of them'). Most of what he says recalls Pearse's oration at the grave of O'Donovan Rossa in August 1915, where he urged the need for military action and sacrificial death in the cause of Irish freedom ('Life springs from death.... Ireland unfree shall never be at peace'). O'Casey might have dramatised the fervent responses of the Speaker's audience to this rhetoric. He had ample historical warrant for doing this. At Rossa's funeral, hundreds of thousands of people listened to Pearse with unalloyed approval. In the words of a contemporary account, with which O'Casey would have been familiar, 'For some moments after Mr. Pearse had finished there was an intense, an all-pervading silence, then we who are accustomed to stand subdued in the home of death gave forth round after round of cheers which must have gladdened the spirits of Rossa and his colleagues.' Instead, he dramatises its effect on Fluther and Peter, whose patriotic fervour is inspired as much by drink as by what they have experienced at the meeting ('they drink and speak with the fullness of emotional passion'). The speeches of Fluther and Peter at this point are parodies of cheap political rhetoric. The militaristic overtones ('Every nerve in me body was quiverin' to do somethin' desperate') can only sound ridiculous given what we know of the two men. The rhetoric of freedom and of political nationalism is exposed to mild ridicule in the following exchange, which makes it impossible to take the earnest pleadings of the orator with proper seriousness.

> **The Covey** (*To the* **Barman**). Two more, please. (*To* ROSIE). Freedom! What's th' use o' freedom, if it's not economic freedom?
> **Rosie** (*emphasizing with extended arm and moving finger*). *I* used them very words just before you come in. "A lot o' thricksters," says I, "that wouldn't know what freedom was if they got it from their mother." . . .
> (*To the* **Barman**). Didn't I, Tommy?
> **Barman**. I disremember.
> **Rosie** (*to the* **Barman**). No, you don't disremember. Remember you said, yourself, it was all "only a flash in th' pan." Well, "flash in th' pan or no flash in th' pan," says I, "they're not goin' to get Rosie Redmond," says I, "to fight for freedom that wouldn't be worth winnin' in a raffle!"

> (Act Two, lines 161-77).

HUMANITY INCOMPATIBLE WITH POLITICAL IDEALISM

Fluther and Peter represent the ridiculous, if harmless, influence of political activity. From O'Casey's point of view, and that of the play, the military figures, Clitheroe, Brennan and Langon, are there to show how a political creed, in this case militant nationalism, can dehumanise its adherents. O'Casey underlines this point as the representatives of the Citizen Army and the Volunteers arrive in the bar room with The Plough and the Stars and the Tricolour, and solemnly dedicate themselves to their abstract cause, at the same time emphasising its absolute priority for them over all merely human relationships ('Ireland is greater than a mother . . . Ireland is greater than a wife'). It is not only the nationalist military figures who sacrifice their humanity to an abstract political ideal. The Covey preaches another kind of political doctrine: Marxist socialism. This doctrine should inspire in its adherents a passionate concern for the plight of the poor and the working-classes and a sense of comradeship with deprived neighbours. The Covey calls people his comrades, but he is distinguished mainly by his bitter personal hostility to everyone about him, and his boring, negative, half-understood political slogans, which can have no possible effect on the people at whom they are directed, and which lead to sterile bickering with Fluther, who, paradoxically, puts into practice the comradeship that The Covey preaches. It is significant that The Covey's best moments in the play come when he abandons his role as political theorist and assumes the humanity which, O'Casey implies, is incompatible with politics. In his comment on Mollser and his moment of concern for Fluther (Act Four, lines 39; 64-6), The Covey shows how the human personality is enhanced when people cease to think of others as abstractions and begin to recognise them as human beings.

The enormous gulf between decent human feeling and politics is made starkly obvious when Captain Brennan, anxious to preserve the purity and integrity of the national cause, orders Clitheroe to shoot those he calls the 'slum lice' who are looting the shops (Act Four, lines 525-32). It is to Clitheroe's credit that he opposes the idea. The 'slum lice' are among the poor people in whose name the militant nationalists have undertaken the Rising. Captain Brennan's political and social outlook does not permit him to see tenement people as fully human; in his mind they are excluded from the category of Irishmen and Irishwomen to whom the 1916 Proclamation was addressed. Brennan's account of poor people as lice is ironic for more than one reason. When the insurrection collapses, he is forced to seek shelter in the tenement among the people he despises ('I'll have to take me chance, an' thry to lie low here for a while'). There is a further irony in the contrast between Brennan's contemptuous verdict on the tenement people and the sentiments of the 1916 Proclamation (mentioned by The Covey in Act Three, line 95), which embodied the sentiments for which the Rising was fought and to which Brennan officially subscribes. The most famous paragraph of the Proclamation, with its admirable egalitarian ideals, is utterly remote from the political and social realities we find in *The Plough and the Stars*:

> The Republic guarantees religious and civil liberty, equal rights and equal opportunities to all its citizens, and declares its resolve to pursue the happiness and prosperity of the whole nation and of all its parts, cherishing all the children of the nation equally, and oblivious of the differences carefully fostered by an alien government, which have divided a minority from the majority in the past.

The moral weight of the play seems to support the notion that if such genuinely human values as family happiness and stability are to prevail, a primary condition is the rejection of political activity; this, in the world imagined by O'Casey, leads only to suffering and death. Those who express political views or who espouse political causes in this play are fanatics (like the Speaker at the meeting); purveyors of empty rhetoric (like Fluther, Peter and Bessie); vain egotists (like Jack Clitheroe), or bores (like The Covey). It is only when they desist from political attitudes that these characters appear fully human. It tells us much about O'Casey's treatment of politics in *The Plough and the Stars* that our most profound sympathies are aroused by those who, like Bessie and Nora, are victims of political activity.

Classifying *The Plough and the Stars*

*T*HE *Plough and the Stars* is not an easy play to classify. The categories commonly invoked by critics — comedy, tragedy, tragi-comedy — do not on their own provide adequate accounts of its overall effect. There are large elements of all these in the play, but there are also large elements of farce, melodrama, the drama of ideas, and some anticipations of the drama of the absurd. O'Casey's early critics also detected the influence of the cinema and the music-hall *revue*, although O'Casey pointed out that he knew nothing about the cinema and had never seen a *revue* in his life. O'Casey himself described his play as a tragedy, but it satisfies few of the criteria traditionally associated with the tragic form. The following is an attempt to isolate some of the main literary forms commonly invoked in discussion of *The Plough and the Stars*.

(A) TRAGEDY

Unless we think of tragedy in terms of some vague and generalised popular definition, as, for example, describing a literary work in which one or more of the characters die in unpleasant or inappropriate circumstances, which features suffering and sorrow on a large scale and which makes us conscious of the miseries of life, *The Plough and the Stars* is not a tragedy. High tragedy as understood by commentators from pre-Christian times to the present day involves a central figure or figures who can command our earnest goodwill, whose actions, purposes or undertakings are really significant, who inhabit a world where these activities necessarily lead to grave spiritual or physical suffering. None of O'Casey's characters in *The Plough and the Stars* has the kind of eminence or greatness of purpose one associates with the central figures in high tragedy. None is an inevitable victim of the human condition as the great tragic characters are, although many are casual victims of local and particular circumstances: the Anglo-Irish conflict, economic conditions in the slums, the 1916 Rising, for example. The fact that O'Casey's characters are socially insignificant does not necessarily disqualify them from being tragic figures: humble people with dignity and high moral worth, whose commitment to a serious purpose inevitably leads to their downfall, could be regarded as fit subjects for tragedy.

Of the characters in *The Plough and the Stars,* Nora Clitheroe comes nearest to being a tragic character. Her absolute devotion to her husband, her refusal to share him with even the noblest cause, provide her with a powerful, even obsessive, sense of purpose. In high tragedy, the sense of doom surrounding the principal characters is present from the beginning; in *The Plough and the Stars* this is hardly the case, since it is quite possible to feel that things might have been otherwise for Nora; she might have persuaded her vacillating husband to remain with her. However much she suffers, Nora does not possess the moral or intellectual stature one expects in a heroine of tragedy. She does not develop in awareness or in recognition of the larger realities around her, as genuinely tragic figures do. On the contrary, she declines in both stature and awareness with the progress of events, ultimately losing all consciousness of the real world. Nora is largely a passive, pathetic victim of circumstances rather than a tragic protagonist. The same is true of Bessie Burgess. There is no sense of tragic inevitability about her death in the last Act; she is killed by a stray bullet which might just as easily have killed Nora. She is the victim of blind chance, not of tragic fate. Like Nora, Bessie lacks the status and dignity of the genuinely tragic figure. She goes to her death without any real understanding of herself or her plight.

(B) COMEDY

It is for its comic elements that *The Plough and the Stars is* most memorable. Its most convincing character, Fluther Good, is the conventional comic buffoon who, like Shakespeare's clowns, is also profoundly wise. Much of the dialogue involves comic exchanges, ranging from downright abuse through sarcasm and irony to subtle humour and wit, and also involving much verbal quibbling. Most of the comic dialogue is sharp-edged because O'Casey's characters are sharp-tongued: they tend to laugh at each other rather than with each other. Comic victims like Peter Flynn are exposed to continuous mockery. His harmless, decorative pose as a patriot is a constant target for his companions. The Covey, in particular, has an ample store of venomous abuse for those he dislikes: he sees Peter as a lunatic 'lashin'' around with a lethal weapon' and 'like th' illegitimate son of an illegitimate child of a corporal in the Mexican army'. Peter, when sufficiently stirred, can reply in kind ('You lean long lanky lath of a lousey bastard'). This kind of broad, crude verbal abuse is, unfortunately, too large a feature of the play, but it is counterbalanced by more subtle effects. Many of these are inspired by O'Casey's understanding of the unaccountable quirks of human nature, and involve situational rather than verbal, comedy. A good example is found in Act Two, when Fluther quixotically defends Rosie Redmond's honour against The Covey's attack and then proceeds to enjoy the lady's favours. Again, in Act Three, Bessie and Mrs. Gogan, not long ago at each other's throats, are united in pride at what they have acquired through looting shops at the height of the battle. Serious people and issues are made to appear ludicrous through incongruous juxtaposition. The solemn, patriotic voice of the silhouetted speaker in Act Two is implicitly mocked by the context in which it is heard: a bar-room brawl involving disputes about respectability and status among tenement women.

The most interesting comic dimension to *The Plough and the Stars* is also one that is found in the modern drama of the absurd, most notably in the plays of Samuel Beckett, featuring events which are simultaneously comic, brutal and horrifying. O'Casey, like Beckett, is able to invoke what Wilson Knight, referring to the grotesque comedy of *King Lear* calls 'a humour that treads the brink of tears, and tragedy which needs but an infinitesimal shift of perspective to disclose the infinitely varied riches of comedy'. In the comic context created by O'Casey, even the cruellest suffering still yields up its own black humour. Mrs. Gogan has for years been watching the slow physical decline of her consumptive daughter Mollser, whose body lies in a coffin on the stage at the beginning of Act Four. Fluther, Peter and The Covey play cards near the coffin. Bessie Burgess feels pity for Mrs. Gogan in her bereavement, but Fluther, who knows his neighbour better, takes a contrary view:

> **Bessie**. Oh, th' poor mother, o' course. God help her, it's a terrible blow to her!
> **Fluther**. A terrible blow? Sure, she's in her element now, woman, mixin' earth to earth, an' ashes t'ashes, an' dust to dust, an' revellin' in plumes an' hearses, last days an' judgements!
>
> (Act Four, lines 304-9)

Death, far from being the ultimate terror, is here seen as a kind of self-enhancing diversion for the bereaved, and Mrs. Gogan's tearful aspect cannot conceal her pride at her sense of the importance of being connected with the death *of* Mollser. Mrs. Gogan is an unwitting source of black comedy as she revels throughout in the contemplation of death and all its fascinating implications. Her lyrical account of her dream featuring a dead Fluther clearly reveals her morbid enjoyment of the experience. Her obsession with the trappings of death is again exposed to ironic contemplation as she watches the dead Bessie and gives a leisurely account of her condition and looks forward to the ritual of laying her out:

Mrs. Gogan (*as she the spreads the sheet*). Oh, God help her, th' poor woman, she's stiffenin' out as hard as she can! Her face has written on it th' shock o' sudden agony, an' her hands is whitenin' into th' smooth shininess of wax.

Nora (*whimperingly*). Take me away, take me away; don't leave me here to be lookin' an' lookin' at it!

Mrs. Gogan (*going over to* **Nora** *and putting her arm round her*). (Come on with me, dear, an' you can doss in poor Mollser's bed, till we gather some neighbours to come an' give th' last friendly touches to Bessie in th' lonely layin' of her out.

(Act Four, lines 652-62)

(C) FARCE

There are large elements of farce in *The Plough and the Stars*. The object of farce is to provoke simple, hearty laughter. It features clowning, buffoonery, exaggerated physical action, often repeated, and exaggerated or caricatured character-types placed in ludicrous situations. It makes use of broad verbal humour and horseplay. It is a low, unsubtle form of comedy. O'Casey's presentation of Peter Flynn, The Covey, Bessie and Mrs. Gogan involves a good deal of farcical business. Much, for example, is made of such trivia as Peter's problems with his collars ('as stiff with starch as a shinin' band o' solid steel'), and of Peter's shirt which is passed around a good deal. Too much is made of the childish conflicts between The Covey and Peter, who, like Bessie and Mrs. Gogan, exchange exaggerated verbal abuse in the true farcical tradition. Horseplay, too, has its place. Peter runs after The Covey with his drawn sword. Fluther and The Covey act as if they are going to fight. Their abortive combat is, however, an exercise in mock-heroics: (Fluther 'suddenly springs into the middle of the shop, flings his hat into the corner, whips off his coat, and begins to paw the air'). Bessie and Mrs. Gogan confront each other menacingly; the former jumps out to face her opponent, who plunges out into the centre of the floor 'in a wild tempest of hysterical rage'. Bessie gives Peter a push that sends him 'tottering to the end of the shop', while the barman pushes the contending women towards the door. In the same scene, a baby is passed from Mrs. Gogan to Peter, who leaves it on the floor, and wants Fluther to take care of it. All of this material belongs to farce rather than to comedy proper.

(D) MELODRAMA

Melodrama is to tragedy as farce is to comedy. It involves the sacrifice of character and of probability to violent effect, and a heightening of the emotional temperature, through sensational action and spectacle. In *The Plough and the Stars,* O'Casey strives for melodramatic effects from time to time. In Act Three, for example, the mortally wounded Lieutenant Langon comes on stage moaning that 'Th' stomach is ripped out o' me', while Nora 'rushes wildly out of the house and flings her arms around the neck of Clitheroe with a fierce and joyous insistence'. From the arrival of Brennan, Clitheroe and the wounded Langon until Clitheroe finally parts from Nora (Act Three, lines 51-673), the action is highly melodramatic. Langon in his dying agony is calling for help. Nora is imploring her husband to stay with her in frenzied tones ('My love for you made me mad with terror'), and he is only able to break free by forcibly loosening her grip on him and pushing her away. The last Act makes an even more melodramatic appeal to the emotions. Two corpses are in a coffin on a darkened stage; one is that of a still-born child, the other of a victim of disease. News of Clitheroe's death is relayed by Brennan in heightened, highly-charged language ('An' then I seen The Plough an' the Stars fallin' like a shot as th' roof crashed in, an' where I'd left poor Jack was nothin' but a leppin spout o' flame'). Nora becomes insane, and Bessie Burgess is shot dead on stage. Much pathos and excitement are extracted from her death, which is enacted in the true melodramatic tradition ('Merciful God, I'm shot, I'm shot! Th' life's pourin' out o' me!').

Style and Language in *The Plough and the Stars*

THE language of *The Plough and the Stars* is compounded of many diverse elements. It is broadly based on the idiom of the Dublin tenement-dwellers who form the majority of O'Casey's characters, and to that extent the style is realistic and colloquial. Some of the earliest objections to O'Casey's play were based on what critics thought of as an unduly crude and earthy use of language, which led some of the actors to refuse to speak certain lines. The cruder elements of the language of the play are found mainly in Rosie Redmond's lines, and in the numerous passages of verbal abuse. These involve most of the characters. The Covey calls Peter a 'little malignant oul' bastard' and 'a lemon-whiskered oul' swine'; Bessie, many of whose speeches are particularly crude, calls Nora a 'little over-dressed throllop'; Clitheroe calls Bessie 'that old bitch'; Bessie describes the Irish patriots as 'lice crawlin' about feedin' on the fatness o' the land'; Fluther calls Covey a 'lowser' who will see 'some snots flyin' around'. This, as O'Casey saw it, was the authentic speech of the tenements, and it forms the bedrock of the style of the play.

O'Casey, however, features other styles and other idioms in *The Plough and the Stars*. Not all the exchanges involve crude verbal abuse. In the love-scene between Jack and Nora in Act One, the language is sentimental, sometimes embarrassingly so ('Little, little red-lipped Nora'). Another kind of sentimentality seizes Peter Flynn as emotion bubbles up in him and Fluther at the meeting: 'I felt a burnin' lump in me throat when I heard th' bard playin' 'The Soldiers' Song'.' The chronically-ill Mollser is invested with a sentimental significance, especially by her mother, Mrs. Gogan. After Mollser's death, for example, Mrs. Gogan tells Fluther that he'll find 'that Mollser, in th' happy place she's gone to, won't forget to whisper, now an' again, th' name o' Fluther'. Again, the language of sentiment is dominant in Captain Brennan's account of Jack Clitheroe's death, which is in the best melodramatic tradition. The speech calls out for musical accompaniment of an appropriately inspirational kind:

> I could do nothin' for him — only watch his
> breath comin' an' goin' in
>   quick, jerky gasps, an' a tiny sthream o' blood
> thricklin' out of his mouth,
>   down over his lower lip.... I said a prayer for th'
> dyin', an' twined his
>   Rosary beads around his fingers.... He took it like
> a man. His last whisper was to 'Tell Nora to be
> brave; that I'm ready to meet my God, an' that I'm
>   proud to die for Ireland'

>   (Act 4, lines 145-63)

DIALOGUE AND VOCABULARY

O'Casey's style in *The Plough and the Stars* is much admired for its richness, exuberance and colour. It is important to recognise the fact that although the dialogue of the play is based on the speech of Dublin tenement-dwellers, the speeches of the characters are not always a faithful transcript of what O'Casey might have heard such characters say in their day-to-day transactions. The vocabulary, idioms and speech-patterns of such people, together with their rich store of imagery, formed the raw material which O'Casey shaped and transformed into something necessarily more artificial and stylised than the colloquial speech of real people. There are, indeed, many times when O'Casey so patterns and heightens his language that many of the speeches become impressive exercises in poetic prose. The part of Bessie Burgess provides an interesting example of this. When the occasion demands, Bessie can be more crude and earthy in her speech than any of the other characters. But she can also move to the opposite extreme. In her more emotional and exalted moments, she speaks the language of the Authorised Version of the Bible, and sounds like an Old Testament figure. Bessie's biblical outpourings are associated with her devotion to the cause of the British Empire. Those who oppose this cause are threatened by her in a confused, though impressive, allusion to Psalm 91: 'But you'll not escape from th' arrow that flieth be night, or th' sickness that wasteth be day.... they'll be scattered abroad, like th' dust in th' darkness.' Again, Bessie has an apocalyptic vision of the young British soldiers 'layin' down their white bodies, shredded into torn an' bloody pieces, on th' altar that God himself has built for th' sacrifice of heroes.' This exalted language is as remote as it could possibly be from Bessie's other idiom ('You bowsey, come in ower that'; 'Th' life's pourin' out o' me. l've got this through you.... through you, you bitch you!').

There is, however, sometimes a common element uniting Bessie's varying uses of language. Consider, for example, her comment on the clothes she and Mrs. Gogan have looted: 'They'll go grand with th' dresses we're after liftin', when we've stitched a sthray bit o' silk to lift th' bodices up a little bit higher, so as to shake th' shame out o' them'. What this passage has in common with the biblical one is its deliberate patterning and conscious use of heavily alliterative effects (*stitched, stray, silk, shake, shame.. bodices, bit*). O'Casey even gives Nora, whose language tends to be commonplace and unimaginative, a biblical idiom when she is overcome with joy at her husband's return: 'God be thanked... be thanked. He has been kind and merciful to his poor handmaiden... My Jack, my own Jack, that I thought was lost is found, that I thought was dead is alive again.' Mrs. Gogan, too, has her biblical moments; she has visions of Fluther's 'shakin' soul moored in th' place where the wicked are at rest and th' weary cease from throublin.' Here, however, O'Casey is exposing Mrs. Gogan to gentle mockery, since she gets her biblical quotation wrong: it is the weary who are at rest and the wicked who cease from troubling.

FLUTHER: CRUDE VERBAL ABUSE

Fluther is the most interesting character in the play from the
point of view of style and language. He has a variety of styles,
and O'Casey extracts comedy from his use and misuse of
language. Like Bessie, Fluther has an impressive line in crude
verbal abuse ('G' way, you wurum'; 'Come on, come on, you
lowser'). Fluther has some pretensions to learning, and this
leads to an incongruous use of language from time to time.
Indeed the misapplication of learned terms and of slightly
unusual words becomes one of Fluther's hallmarks: 'Then
Fluther has a vice-versa opinion of them that put ivy-leaves
into their prayer-books'; 'I wasn't goin' to let meself be
malignified by a chancer. He got a little bit too derogatory for
Fluther.' Fluther's fondness for the learned word, which he
sometimes gets right and sometimes not, is part of his *persona*;
it helps to place him as a character, and gives him a distinctive
presence. When he wants to warn The Covey to speak politely,
he tells him to put 'a christianable consthruction on things';
when he expresses doubts about the picture of the sleeping
Venus, he says that 'It's nearly a derogatory thing to be in the
room where it is; and when he dismisses the notion that a loud
voice signifies a large brain, he declares that 'shoutin's no
manifestin' forth of a growin' mind'.

Fluther's language, like Bessie's, is a compound of
incongruous elements. Consider, for example, his rebuke to the
atheism of The Covey: 'You'll be kickin' an' yellin' for th' priest,
yet, me boyo. I'm not goin' to stand silent an' simple listenin' to
a thick like you makin' a maddenin' mockery o' God Almighty'.
There is an interesting interplay here between the mainly
colloquial vocabulary (*kickin'*; *yellin'*; *boyo'*) and the formalised
rhythms of the speech, the carefully contrived alliterative
effects ('stand silent an' simple listenin'; 'makin' a maddenin'
mockery'). There are times when O'Casey makes Fluther speak
a perfectly idiomatic language, free of his usual idiosyncrasies.
The most notable example is his witty comment on the respect
due to religion: 'I think we ought to have as great a regard for
religion as we can, so as to keep it out of as many things as
possible'.

A LINGUISTIC SAMENESS

Fluther and Bessie are not the only characters whose speech is colourful and contrived. It is one of the limitations of O'Casey's use of language as a means of characterisation that too many of his characters speak in the same idiom. Peter, for example, a silly, unintelligent character, can still express himself with as much vigour and style as Fluther: 'She makes these collars as stiff with starch as a shinin' band of solid steel'. Here we find the same riotous indulgence in alliteration as we found in the speeches of Bessie and Fluther. The Covey, too, is sometimes given the same linguistic patterns, the same alliterative effects, as the other characters. 'It's not long since', he declares, 'th' fathers o' some o' them crawled out o' th' shelterin' slime o' the sea'. The result of all this is a certain linguistic sameness from one speech to the next. Every character tends to sound much like every other one, and apart from Fluther's few stock-phrases which are unmistakably his (for him things are 'derogatory' or 'vice versa'), and Bessie's occasional biblical sallies, O'Casey has failed to individualise his characters through language or imagery. He makes one attempt to represent a use of language by a character other than a tenement-dweller (if we exclude the British soldiers) and this is a failure. In Act Three, he introduces a woman from Rathmines, and makes her speak in a parodied version of a 'superior' accent: 'I was foolish enough to visit a friend, thinking the howl thing was a joke, and now I cawn't get a car or a tram to take me home... a bullet whizzed past within an inch of my nowse'. This is embarrassing, silly and pointless, and merely illustrates O'Casey's uncertainty in dealing with people outside the social circle he understood best. He is successful with the Pearse figure, the Voice of the man, but this is because here he uses the actual words of Pearse. (For an explanation of the presence in the play of the woman from Rathmines, see Critical Comment, No 15).

There is no denying the liveliness and colour of O'Casey's language, and the vigour and energy of his style. It is easy to imagine the delight actors take in speaking their lines. The problem with O'Casey's dramatic language, however, lies not in any lack of power or imaginative force in the speeches, but in the fact that so many of the characters speak in much the same way; for most of the time O'Casey seems unable to give his characters a distinctive idiom. A good test of this for those who are familiar with the play is to try to identify the speakers of each of the following:

(a) You mind your own business ma'am, an' stupefy your foolishness be gettin' dhrunk.

(b) Isn't it a nice thing to be listenin' to a lassie an' hangin' our heads in dead silence, knowin' that some persons think more of a ball of malt than they do of th' blessed saints.

(c) If the two of yous don't thry to make a generous altheration in your goin's on an' keep on thryin' t' inaugurate th' customs o' th' rest o' th' house into this place, yous can flit into other lodgin's where your bowsey battlin' 'ill meet, maybe, with an encore.

(d) If I was you, Mrs. Gogan, I'd parry her jabbin' remarks be a powerful silence that'll keep her tantalisin' words from penethratin' into your feelin's. It's always betther to leave these people to th' vengeance o' God.

The speakers are Bessie, Mrs. Gogan, Nora and Peter respectively, but this could not easily be deduced from the idiom employed. The first two speeches might easily be interchanged between Bessie and Mrs. Gogan, the third is not typical of Nora's colourless speeches elsewhere in the scene, while the fourth might just as easily belong to Fluther as to Peter.

Fluther is perhaps the most clearly realised and distinctive character in the play from the point of view of style and language. In the end, however, one can grow a little weary of Fluther's idiom, based as it is on the repetition of the same words and phrases ('derogatory' and 'vice versa' being the commonest); on massive alliterative effects such as 'Is a man fermentin' with fear to stick th' showin' off to him of a thing that looks like a shinin' shroud', and 'It would take something more than a thing like you to flutther a feather o' Fluther'. O'Casey is so pleased with this last example that he repeats it within forty lines ('There's no necessity to flutther yourself when you're with Fluther'). These are clever, but like many of O'Casey's effects, they depend on a few obvious devices: particularly word-play and the piling up of alliteration ('flutther/Fluther'). O'Casey also relies on the recurring use of key words which have heavily 'poetic' overtones: *shining*; *dread*; *darkness*; *death*; *shroud*. There is also a heavy dependence on what Raymond Williams has called O'Casey's 'adjectival drunkenness' as exemplified in such continuous effects as 'th' innocent light o' th' shinin' stars' and 'you little sermonizing, little yella-faced, little consequential, little pudgy little bum you'. There is, of course, a diverting comic incongruity in the accumulation of nine adjectival qualifiers for so humble a word as 'bum', and the bathos is impressive.

Whatever objections may be made to O'Casey's language in *The Plough and the Stars*, even its sternest critics will admit that it has the ring of truth, after a certain necessary heightening and colouring have been allowed for. The main weaknesses arise when O'Casey strains too much for effect, when restraint would have better served his purposes. An example of this is the language of the scene in Act Three in which Jack and Nora part for good. Here O'Casey's style is close to that of the popular novelette; it is trite and melodramatic ('O Jack, I gave you everything you asked of me.... Don't fling me from you now').

Examining the Play

A)   FOR DETAILED DISCUSSION

ACT 1

1   What do the stage directions at the beginning of Act One tell us about the kind of people the Clitheroes are?

2   What impressions do you form of (a) Fluther Good and (b) Peter Flynn from reading O'Casey's descriptions of them at the beginning of Act one? Are your early impressions of the two characters confirmed by their later appearances in the play?

3   Before Nora Clitheroe appears on stage, we are given various impressions of her character. Describe these. Are Fluther and Mrs. Gogan fair to Nora and Jack?

4   Why do Mrs. Gogan and Fluther find Peter 'a funny-looking little man'?

5   Fluther and Mrs. Gogan both cast doubt on Jack Clitheroe's motives for joining the Citizen Army. Are they being fair to him? Consider their comments in the light of Clitheroe's subsequent conduct.

6   In what way is Mrs. Gogan's emphasis on Fluther's cough typical of her general outlook? Give examples from other parts of the play.

7   How does The Covey's outlook on public affairs differ from that of the other characters in the Act?

8   Consider the overall significance of The Covey's suggestion that 'there's no such thing as an Irishman'.

9   Explain The Covey's references to 'mollycewels an' atoms' (line 324) and to Adam and Eve and 'th' skeleton of th' man o' Java' (line 358). What is the connection between these references and his argument about the insignificance of nationality?

10   What problems do Peter and The Covey present to Nora?

11   What significance is to be attached to Nora's having a new lock put on her door?

12   Describe the opening impression made by Bessie Burgess.

13   Why does Bessie not appear to like Nora?

14   In what respects does Bessie differ from her neighbours?

15   Try to account for Clitheroe's attitude to Captain Brennan (lines 637-41).

16 Explain why The Covey thinks that Brennan and the others are bringing disgrace on the Citizen Army flag (line 645).
17 What is the tone of The Covey's remarks about 'Ireland's warriors passin' by' (line 659)?
18 How would you describe the relationship between Jack and Nora on the evidence of lines 712-820?
19 Consider the dramatic significance of Captain Brennan's entrance.
20 Describe the effect of Captain Brennan's news of Jack. How can this effect be explained?
21 Discuss some of the ironies implicit in Bessie's final comment (lines 953-59). Comment on the style of her speech.

ACT 2

1 What is the effect of Rosie's words (lines 30-39) on our attitude to the participants in the patriotic meeting?
2 Do you think we are meant to approve of the sentiments of the anonymous Speaker (lines 54-61)?
3 What effect does the context in which they are spoken have on the words of this Speaker?
4 Examine the connection between alcohol and patriotism in *The Plough and the Stars*.
5 Are the patriotic sentiments expressed by Fluther and Peter sincere? Give reasons for your answer.
6 Does O'Casey convey the impression that for some of his characters at least, rousing speech is a substitute for action? Explain your answer.
7 What does his encounter with Rosie tell us about the character of The Covey?
8 Why is it difficult to take seriously The Covey's pronouncements on social and economic issues in this Act?
9 What are the aims of The Foresters, the body to which Peter belongs. Why is he exposed to so much ridicule?
10 Explain Bessie's reference to 'poor little Catholic Belgium' (line 281). Comment on the irony of this reference.
11 'When I think of all the problems in front o' th' workers, it makes me sick to be lookin' at oul' codgers goin' about dhressed up like green-accoutered figures gone asthray out of a toyshop!' Do you think The Covey's comment is fair? What is his solution to the problems facing the workers?

12 Mrs. Gogan's language to Bessie sounds dangerously aggressive. Is there any evidence in the play to suggest that such outbursts are not to be taken seriously?

13 Examine the elements of farce in Act Two.

14 Fluther claims to have received wounds in the service of the Labour movement. Do you believe him?

15 Fluther tells The Covey: 'Don't be comradin' me mate. I'd be on me last legs if I wanted you for a comrade'. Consider the significance of this remark. What does it tell us about the success of the principles for which The Covey stands?

16 Can you account for Fluther's protective attitude towards Rosie (lines 561-70)?

17 Jack Clitheroe declares that 'Ireland is greater than a wife'. Consider this as an expression of the central theme of *The Plough and the Stars*.

18 O'Casey juxtaposes scenes of intense patriotic fervour with episodes of bawdy comedy and farce. What is the effect of this ? How does it reflect O'Casey's dramatic purposes?

ACT 3

1 Why do you think O'Casey introduced Mollser as a character in the play? What is her function?

2 Mrs. Gogan's speech (lines 46-57) gives us a new view of Fluther. Explain.

3 Mrs. Cogan is surprised that Fluther and The Covey are 'pullin' together'. Can you account for their newly-found unity?

4 Discuss Mrs. Cogan's preoccupation with death.

5 Do you find Fluther an unlikely hero?

6 Explain Bessie's response to the events reported by The Covey and Fluther.

7 'If they were fightin' for any thing worthwhile, I wouldn't mind' (lines 194-5). Does this comment represent the overall verdict of the play on the Rising of 1916?

8 Explain Nora's attitude to her husband's participation in the Rising.

9 Mention some of the incidents and comments which suggest that despite all the aggressive talk and quarrelling which mark the lives of the tenement-dwellers, they are good neighbours at heart.

10 Does it surprise you that Bessie is among those who have taken part in looting?

11 The episode involving the lost woman from Rathmines (lines 329-68) is one of the weakest in the play. Why?
12 Why do Bessie and Mrs. Gogan suddenly become firm friends (lines 483-502)?
13 Captain Brennan wanted Clitheroe to kill the looters, whom he calls 'slum lice' (line 531). Comment on the irony of this.
14 Examine the effect of Bessie's comments on Captain Brennan and his occupation (line 554 ff.).
15 Do you feel sympathy for Clitheroe as Nora tries to persuade him to stay with her (lines 579-671)?
16 Is Nora being unfair to her husband in trying to detain him? Explain.
17 What is your final impression of Jack Clitheroe as he leaves Nora?
18 Bessie begins to emerge in a new light as Act Three draws to a close. Explain.

ACT 4

1 Describe the atmosphere suggested by the stage-directions at the beginning of Act Four.
2 How does this Act differ from the previous ones in mood and atmosphere?
3 What is the significance of the card-playing?
4 Examine O'Casey's juxtaposition of the events of everyday life with the horrors of war and domestic tragedy.
5 Discuss Bessie's role in this Act. How has she changed in the course of the play?
6 Does Captain Brennan appear to be a coward in this Act?
7 Consider the irony of Captain Brennan's claim that 'Mrs. Clitheroe's grief will be a joy when she realises that she has had a hero for a husband' (lines 165-6). Does the play as a whole make us see Clitheroe as a hero?
8 Why does O'Casey emphasize Nora's insanity?
9 Why does Fluther think that Mrs. Gogan is 'in her element' (line 306) now that Mollser is dead?
10 The exchanges between Corporal Stoddart and The Covey on the relationship between socialism and patriotic duty have an important bearing on one of the central themes of the play. Explain.

11 Consider the proposition that Fluther and Bessie are the moral heroes of the play.
12 Bessie is indignant when Corporal Stoddart assumes that she is a Sinn Féin supporter. She proceeds to declare her allegiance to Britain (lines 391-400). Consider the irony of her declaration in the light of later events.
13 Fluther defends the 1916 Volunteers against Sergeant Tinley's accusations that they fought unfairly (lines 484-9). In what ways are Fluther's comments on this topic representative of the general attitude of the play? Does O' Casey generally present the men of 1916 in a favourable light?
14 Bessie's death is fraught with irony. Explain.
15 What impression of the British soldiers is conveyed in Act Four?
16 The British soldiers sing 'Keep the 'ome fires burning' in the dead Bessie's living room. Comment on the irony of this.

B)   FOR GENERAL DISCUSSION

1 The other tenement-dwellers, whatever their faults, protect and comfort Nora in her trouble, and with a real effort they preserve a sense of community feeling in the midst of chaos.
2 A bold summary of the events of the play might make it sound intensely bleak, but it is also intensely funny. The swings from pathos to melodrama and farce are extreme, but the wildness, the exuberance, the wit, humour and sentimentality are all parts of O'Casey's vision of life.
3 *The Plough and the Stars* is a play about ordinary people caught up in events and movements beyond their control.
4 The nationalists who rioted in the Abbey in 1926 were not wrong in seeing the play as an attack on the militaristic ideals which inspired the Rising.
5 The main fault with the play is its sentimentality; its main virtue is its humour.
6 In *The Plough and the Stars*, it is the characters who are least puffed up with heroism who are the heroes.

7 *The Plough and the Stars* is a powerful exposure of the random suffering inflicted by the myth and the rhetoric of violence.

8 Very little work is done, or even talked about, in O'Casey's working-class drama.

9 *The Plough and the Stars* offers not the slightest hint of an answer to the terrible problems it raises; O'Casey's entire approach is destructive and negative. The failures and braggarts, the absence of a hero or of a serious political thinker reflect O'Casey's cynicism.

10 *The Plough and the Stars* consists of an unresolved dialogue between Irish nationalism and socialism, in which the representatives of neither side are particularly endearing.

11 In *The Plough and the Stars,* it is not the abstract ideas that matter in the end, but the human qualities of ordinary people.

12 O'Casey's play suggests, in symbolic form, the tragedy of Ireland itself, where heroism and greed, idealism and vainglory, vision and vice, beauty and foulness, poetry and profanity, are inextricably mingled.

13 The comedy of *The Plough and the Stars* comes from pretentiousness, especially in the good-for-nothing, self-regarding men, whose adaptation to environment depends on this comic self-deception. The tragedy is more especially that of the women, caught in a political struggle they are not responsible for and not committed to, but which crushes them none the less.

14 The honesty and compassion of the female characters in the play stands in obvious contrast to the vanity, equivocation and selfishness of the male ones.

15 Since the problems of the slum-dwellers are more personal than national, it is natural that they should be indifferent to patriotic rhetoric.

16 In *The Plough and the Stars,* O'Casey offers no coherent or convincing view of the great issues he raises. All we get are contradictory impressions.

17 If the play has anything positive to suggest, and this is doubtful, it is that humane feelings, kindness, generosity and co-operation, should displace political activity.

18 In *The Plough and the Stars*, commonplace characters become heroic, while those with heroic pretensions become commonplace.

19 The play suggests that O'Casey is at heart a satirist. His most interesting effects are negative and destructive.

20 In *The Plough and the Stars,* the men are largely ineffectual dreamers and idealists, while the women are realists.

Critical Comment

1 After Synge's death in 1909, the reputation of the Abbey Theatre and of the Irish drama was sustained by Seán O'Casey, whose most famous plays — *The Shadow of a Gunman* (1923), *Juno and the Paycock* (1924) and *The Plough and the Stars* (1926), were all produced there. Like Synge, O'Casey was of Protestant parentage and he was intimately and passionately concerned with the Irish nationalist movement. The three plays are set in Dublin slum tenements, and dramatise the desperation of poverty and the confused and violent dissensions of the Irish movements – nationalist and socialist, loyalist and rebellious, Protestant and Catholic, which gave this desperation its peculiar terror. He knew his characters as one of themselves and presented them with humour and compassion, mingling their degradation, absurdity and pathos with their dignity and intermittent grandeur. As documents, the plays are moving records of Irish suffering, and something more, for they anticipate the squalid and terrifying urban wars that have become the nightmares of great cities in the second half of the century. °

Christopher Gillie

2 O'Casey's earliest and best plays, *Juno and the Paycock, The Shadow of a Gunman,* and the splendid *The Plough and the Stars* (this was the flag of the Citizen Army) are essentially tragedies. 'They are shot through, nevertheless, with a broad, deep and effective humour — the vital humour of the Irish poor. The Irish 'troubles' give O'Casey a background which enables him to introduce plausibly the acts of violence which he needs to resolve, in a tragic sense, which otherwise might be merely static scenes of pathos or humour. Thus the atmosphere of these wonderful plays is sometimes like that of a music-hall cross-talk (but of a kind that could only be invented by a man of genius) interrupted by a murder. Like Synge, the young O'Casey listened to the language of the Irish poor, but looked not for beautiful cadences, only for the unmistakable ring of truth.

G.S. Fraser

3 Each of O'Casey's three great plays, *The Shadow of a Gunman, Juno and the Paycock* and *The Plough and the Stars*, is set in the poorer parts of the city in which the playwright was born; in each there is a background of armed fighting and revolutionary catchcries. A writer using such material starts with an initial advantage. His theme is the impact of war and of a national ideal embodying courage and self-sacrifice on lives that would otherwise be merely sordid and lacking in dramatic interest. All these plays verge on melodrama, but the intensity of a real experience, which was shared by the author and his early audiences, saves them from being quite that. The dominant motif is pity, pity for suffering humanity. The necessity of the national struggle is accepted; it is felt to be as inevitable as birth or death. Yet the heroes of these plays are not its soldiers, but their womenfolk who show courage of a different sort — who fight without sentiment and without conscious idealism to aid the suffering and afflicted, and to protect their own.

Grattan Freyer

4 A stranger to Ireland and her tumultuous history might
well ask why *The Plough and the Stars* caused such an
indignant reaction. In *The Plough,* the background is
the Easter Rising of 1916; an event that had assumed a
semi-legendary, semi-religious significance. The blood-
sacrifice of Pádraig Pearse, James Connolly and the
other leaders had become the symbol of Ireland's age-
long struggle for freedom. It was both a crucifixion and
a resurrection. By depicting the participants, not as
heroes but as human beings subject to the fears, the
pomps and vanities of the flesh, and by showing the
ordinary Dubliners as indifferent, or hostile, or having a
glorious jamboree pillaging the shops, the play seemed
to ardent patriots, especially those whose menfolk had
perished in the event, to be a deliberate attempt to
debunk the spirit that had inspired and uplifted those
who took part.

Hugh Hunt

5 In the light of O'Casey's consistent refusal to idealize
violence, it was no surprise that *The Plough and the
Stars* provoked a riot in the Abbey Theatre when groups
of diehard nationalists interrupted the performance
with a wild demonstration against his ironic treatment
of the Easter Rising. According to the outraged rioters,
O'Casey had insulted the nation by deflating the
patriots and concentrating on his own working-class
Dublin, especially the tragi-comic men, women and
children of the now bullet-riddled tenements. He was
also accused of desecrating the sacred Republican flag
by allowing it to be brought into a pub, and of defiling
the honour of Irish womanhood by portraying an Irish
girl as a prostitute. Furthermore, in the second Act the
actual words of the martyred Pádraig Pearse had been
exposed to mock-heroic irony. While the messianic
Pearse-figure is outside the pub calling on the people to
join him in a ritualistic blood-sacrifice, preaching his

sermon on 'the sanctity of bloodshed' and 'the exhilaration of war', the earthy characters of the slums are inside the pub drinking and brawling in a series of farcical battles about respectability. Throughout the play, the frailty and humanity of these magnificently rude mechanicals, led by Fluther Good, Jinnie Gogan, Bessie Burgess, Peter Flynn and The Covey, mock the holiness of the war.

David Krause

6 *The Plough and the Stars* has a cinematic quality. Unity of place is abandoned, with scenes in the street and pub as well as in two of the rooms of the tenement. Violent actions take place before the audience, instead of offstage as in the earlier plays. Yet the physical breadth does not diffuse the theme — the subversion of creative human relationships by fanatical patriotism and what passes for the 'noble cause'. In *The Plough and the Stars* the truly brave are those who are unwittingly drawn into the holocaust, and perform humane actions through ordinary kindness or goodness of heart. The play's main fault is a sentimentality amounting to mawkishness in an early scene between Jack and Nora.

Christopher Fitz-Simon

7 This brings us to O'Casey's anti-heroes or clowns, men like Fluther Good, The Covey and Peter Flynn — cowards and braggarts who manage to temper their folly with an instinctive shrewdness and wisdom that is attractive and reprehensible and human. They are unable to wage a private war against the Irish establishment. They have been trapped in their Dublin tenements by a lifetime of poverty and hunger, and now by the terror of the revolution. They are only free in their own conception of themselves, in their eloquent lies and fantasies, in their selfish preservation of their lives in a ridiculous and dangerous world. Their guile and bravado, their comic defences, function best in a spirit of anarchy and belligerent imagination. Their own type of guerrilla warfare must be fought with words and mother-wit, the only weapons of the dispossessed, and therefore, their lyrical and over-leaping rhetoric provides a vicarious gratification of their impossible dreams.

David Krause

8 Like so many of O'Casey's women, Nora knows the terror and the suffering that lie behind the drunken idealism of the men, and Nora is one of O'Casey's great truth-tellers. Like Little Mollser who wonders if there is a titter of sense anywhere in Dublin, Nora is crushed by her existence, but O'Casey's theme in the play is something more than individual helplessness. Many dramatists have argued our helplessness, but O'Casey argues also a way beyond helplessness, the way of creating a decent community of support and sympathy, even in the worst of times. Uncle Peter's nationalism is a silly charade; the young Covey's socialism is a front for his own insecurity; Jack's patriotism comes out of a mixture of motives, but Bessie Burgess and Fluther Good show us that decent realists can, in a small and limited way, make a better world than any Nationalist or Socialist dreamer. Together they protect and succour Nora, and with real effort they maintain a sense of community in the midst of chaos, and the final failure of their efforts does not invalidate their worth.

Richard Fallis

9 O'Casey's plays lack form, lack movement and in the final analysis lack any informing purpose. To this day I do not know just where the author's sympathies lie. O'Casey offers no solution; he proposes no remedy; he suggests no hope.

Joseph Wood Krutch

10 So far as the politics presented in the plays concern the liberation of Ireland by force, O'Casey's personal disillusionment with the whole programme accounts for its sardonic, negative treatment: of Pearse's mystical rhetoric of blood-letting, the bombast of Peter Flynn and all the other hangers-on. Jack Clitheroe has joined the Citizen Army out of vanity. The failures and braggarts, the absence of any hero, or of a serious political thinker, reflect O'Casey's cynicism. The question is whether it leads into a series of culs-de-sac, admitting possible answers only to dally with and retreat from them. If the women, as guides to an ameliorating domestic private sanctuary, in the end default, so too do Nationalist politics as a route to society's discovering a coherent sense of itself. Everything, it might be argued, ends in 'chassis' because set to work in a dramatic world dishonestly constructed to admit no real adversary. The question arises even more pressingly when we look at how the plays deal with ideas which O'Casey did actually profess. O'Casey did believe, 'There's only one freedom for th' workin' man: conthrol o' th' means o' production, rates of exchange, an' th' means of distribution' — and gives the words to a windbag [The Covey].

D.E.S. Maxwell

11 Larkin's people for some time have been making war on the Irish Volunteers. I think this is largely inspired by a disgruntled fellow named O'Casey. By this attitude they have antagonised the sympathy of all sections of the country and none more than the advanced section.

Thomas Clarke (the 1916 leader)

12 Seán O'Casey, who retained an affection for Pearse, had grave doubts about his influence on the workers of Dublin, and brought down a storm of abuse on his own head when, in 1926, the Abbey produced his play, *The Plough and the Stars*. Demonstrating the futility of death — even noble death — it dramatised the effect of Pearse's words on the emotional tenement-dwellers of his Dublin. The reaction of Fluther Good, a carpenter, to the stirring words of Pearse at the grave of Wolfe Tone shows how O'Casey, after the Civil War, felt about the rhetoric of blood.... Not until recently have Irish writers again questioned the Pearse myth seriously.

Ruth Dudley Edwards

13 Many of you have been tempted to join the much talked-of Irish Volunteer movement by the wild impulse of genuine enthusiasm. You have again allowed yourselves to be carried away by words — words — words. You have momentarily forgotten that there can be no interests outside those identified with your own class. Workers, this movement is built on a reactionary basis. Are you going to be satisfied with a crowd of chattering well-fed aristocrats and commercial bugs? Are you going to rope Ireland's poor outside the boundaries of the Nation?

Seán O'Casey in *The Irish Worker,* January 1914

14 When Seán O'Casey died in 1964, he had behind him close on thirty years as an avowed Communist, and twenty more as a labour sympathiser. There are, however, very few socialist characters in his plays. In *The Plough and the Stars* we have The Covey. Many of us have met him. He is the dogmatic, self-proclaimed Marxist, who speaks in technicalities because, not really understanding the creed he professes, he cannot explain it in common or ordinary language.

C. Desmond Greaves

15 In the second Act of *The Plough* — the scene in the pub — which many regard as the best piece of dramaturgy that O'Casey ever devised, there is a gorgeous barging match between two ladies (Bessie Burgess and Mrs. Gogan). At this point in the play, one of the actresses refused to play the part at all, whereat Seán, ever kindly disposed towards his players, very decently wrote in a small new role for the offended party — that of an upper-class lady from Rathmines who had lost her way in the tumult and could find nobody to conduct her home. This character had nothing to do with the rest of the play, but was written in purely to keep a distressed lady with a part in the play. And she is still there to this day, often to the puzzlement of literary commentators who cannot see any point in her being there at all.

Denis Johnston

16 *The Plough and the Stars* is the one play in which O'Casey manages to bring political complexities and moral insight successfully together. The last scene, in which the British Tommies sing 'Keep the 'ome fires burning' in the dead Bessie's living-room, is O'Casey's most powerful image of the vicious collusion which has taken place between domestic, homely bliss and political and military violence. Outside Dublin burns. But it is an odd city. It is a metaphorical space in which the virtues of humanity confront the vices of politics . . . It is a city in which we have had Pearse's ferocious political rhetoric juxtaposed with Rosie Redmond's humanity, much to Pearse's dramatic discomfiture. There Jack Clitheroe has died out of simple egoism and bravura, and not for any political ideal. It is not a city in which politics has any truly social or human basis. Instead, only in repudiation of politics can humanity express itself.... The form of the play, moulded by its familiar tenement setting, is the form dictated by a moralist's desire to replace politics by an alternative human system.... What O'Casey has done here is to cast politics in the role of an inexorable fate which exploits the flaws in men's characters for the sake of destroying them.

Seamus Deane

17 The distance between the language of O'Casey and the language of poetic drama is considerable; but perhaps a more significant distance is that between his language and that of Synge. It is not a simple difference of status between the two as writers, although Synge's sensibility is clearly the finer. It is also a change in the language of society, a change from the speech of isolated peasants and fishermen, where dignity and vitality of language were directly based on an organic living process, to the speech of townsmen, normally colourless and drab, containing the undiscriminated rhythms of the scriptures, popular hymns, and commercial songs, which, when it wishes to be impressive, must become either drunken or hysterical, and end in extravagance. When O'Casey brings on two of his people with the note 'Emotion is bubbling up in them, so that when they drink and when they speak, they drink and speak with the fullness of emotional passion', he is at once diagnosing the secret of his impressive language and blustering about it, for the point is that the men are simply drunk. To speak, as townsmen, in the way they do, they would have to be. Colour, that is to say, needs to be artificially infused, just as O'Casey takes care to relieve the drabness of contemporary clothes with one or two characters appearing in fancy dress (Peter, in *The Plough and the Stars*, wears the green and white uniform of The Foresters).

Raymond Williams

Selected Bibliography

BIOGRAPHY

Seán O'Casey, Hugh Hunt, Gill's Irish Lives, 1980.

CRITICISM

A Critical History of Modern Irish Drama 1891-1980, D.E.S. Maxwell, 1984.

English Drama from Ibsen to Eliot, Raymond Williams, 1964.

The Irish Theatre, Christopher Fitz-Simon, Thames and Hudson, 1983.

The Irish Renaissance, Richard Fallis, Syracuse University Press, 1977.

The Modern Age (Volume 7 of *The Pelican History of English Literature*), Pelican, 1961.

Movements in English Literature 1900-1940, Christopher Gillie, Cambridge University Press, 1975.

The Modern Writer and His World, G. S. Fraser, Penguin, 1965.

The O'Casey Enigma, ed. M. Ó hAodha, Mercier Press, 1980.

Seán O'Casey, The Man and His Work, David Krause, Thames and Hudson, 1960.